Pearson

At Pearson, we have a simple mission: to help people make more of their lives through learning.

We combine innovative learning technology with trusted content and educational expertise to provide engaging and effective learning experiences that serve people wherever and whenever they are learning.

From classroom to boardroom, our curriculum materials, digital learning tools and testing programmes help to educate millions of people worldwide – more than any other private enterprise.

Every day our work helps learning flourish, and wherever learning flourishes, so do people.

To learn more, please visit us at **www.pearson.com**

Impact

—

Do more with less

Jo Owen

Pearson

Harlow, England • London • New York • Boston • San Francisco • Toronto • Sydney
Dubai • Singapore • Hong Kong • Tokyo • Seoul • Taipei • New Delhi
Cape Town • São Paulo • Mexico City • Madrid • Amsterdam • Munich • Paris • Milan

PEARSON EDUCATION LIMITED
KAO Two
KAO Park
Harlow CM17 9NA
United Kingdom
Tel: +44 (0)1279 623623
Web: www.pearson.com

First edition published 2025 (print and electronic)

© Pearson Education Limited 2025 (print and electronic)

ISBN: 978-1-292-47689-6 (print)
           978-1-292-74479-7 (ePub)

British Library Cataloguing-in-Publication Data
A catalogue record for the print edition is available from the British Library

Library of Congress Cataloging-in-Publication Data
A catalog record for the print edition is available from the Library of Congress

10 9 8 7 6 5 4 3 2 1
29 28 27 26 25

Cover design by [Two Associates]

Print edition typeset in Charter ITC Pro 10/14 by Straive
Printed in the UK by Bell and Bain Ltd, Glasgow

NOTE THAT ANY PAGE CROSS REFERENCES REFER TO THE PRINT EDITION

Contents

—

About the author

Jo Owen is a founder of eight NGOs with a combined turnover of more than £100 million annually, including Teach First which became the UK's largest graduate recruiter. He has also built a business in Japan, started a bank, was a partner at Accenture, been sued for $12 billion, and was head of research for a political party at Westminster. He started his career in brand management at P&G and holds degrees from Cambridge University and London Business School. He was awarded an OBE by the Queen in 2015.

Jo is the only person to receive the Chartered Management Institute Gold Award four times for his books, which include *How to Lead*, *Global Teams* and *Resilience*, all published by Pearson. His books have been published in over 100 editions in 30 foreign languages.

Introduction and summary

The impact challenge

This book answers a very simple question: how do you really make things happen?

Managers used to have it easy. Your job would have been to make things happen through people you controlled. You would pass orders down the hierarchy and information back up the hierarchy. Everyone knew their role, and everyone knew their place. That world has disappeared along with the suit, bowler hat and briefcase.

Your job is no longer to make things happen through people you control. You have to make things happen through people you do *not* control, or do not want to be controlled. That changes everything. Management has become far more challenging and rewarding than ever before.

You have to gain the support of colleagues in other departments, senior managers, and perhaps

> **Management has become far more challenging and rewarding than ever before**

customers, suppliers and other stakeholders as well. Even your own team probably does not want to be micromanaged. As professionals, they want to be trusted to do the job themselves. They do not want to be told what to do.

This loss of control is liberating. In the past, your power and your ability to make things happen was dictated by your position in the hierarchy. The higher you climbed, the more you could do. Your power was the formal power that came with your position. If you had more budget, more decision-making rights and a bigger team you could do more. If you lacked budget, decision-making rights or team then you could do very little beyond what you were told to do.

Formal power that comes with your position still matters. But formal power is no longer enough. You need to amplify your formal power with informal power. Informal power is the sort of power which enables you to:

- find the resources to achieve your goals;
- gain the support of top management for your ideas;
- build a network of allies within and beyond the firm who want to help you;
- become the team member or manager of choice;
- make sure you work on assignments which will help you grow and develop;
- receive more recognition;
- overcome resistance to change and to your initiatives;
- survive the next restructuring;
- achieve influence across the organisation;
- control your destiny rather than be controlled by the organisation;
- bypass formal procedures which normally block you;
- gain the promotion you deserve.

As you look around your own organisation, you can probably see colleagues who make things happen and have influence far beyond their formal role. You can also see many other colleagues who make more modest contributions because they feel constrained by their formal role and formal power.

The purpose of this book is to show how you can have impact at scale, even when you have little in the way of formal power. And if you have some formal power, this book will show you how you can have even greater impact and achieve even more by using informal power to amplify your formal power.

Summary and key lessons of the book

If you want to do more with less, you have to invest in building your social capital so that people will want to work with you and help you. This is where the book starts:

Chapter 1: 'Become the colleague of choice'. This lays the groundwork for doing more with less. When people want to work with you, you can achieve far more than when they are forced to work with you. You acquire this social capital by building trust. This is not just about being credible and doing as you say. It is also about being selfless and helping others so that they will want to help you. This is a new world in which givers, not takers, succeed in the long term.

> **This is a new world in which givers, not takers, succeed in the long term**

Chapter 2: 'Weave your web' helps you map out who you need in your power network to make things happen. Become the colleague of choice with the right colleagues at all levels. Two people are central to your web. The first is your manager: by learning to manage your manager, you learn how to manage anyone. The second key colleague you need is a sponsor: this is the senior executive who will look out for you. Sponsors are vital, because all the big decisions about your career will be taken when you are not in the room: who will be in the room rooting for you when

> **All the big decisions about your career will be taken when you are not in the room**

those decisions are made? This chapter shows how to find and use your sponsor.

Chapter 3: 'Work smart, not just hard'. If you want to have an impact, you have to work on the right agenda. Never mistake activity for achievement: it is possible to be very busy and stressed dealing with the noise of corporate life, without achieving anything. With the right agenda, you will discover that you acquire power and influence; people will want to work with you; you develop the mindset and habits of the best leaders. This chapter shows how you can find and develop the right agenda, regardless of where you are in the organisation. Learn to make the agenda, not take the agenda.

Learn to make the agenda, not take the agenda

Chapter 4: 'Make it happen'. If you have the right agenda and right network, you still need to make things happen. This short chapter reviews the basics of productivity and then shows that the most productive people do not rely much (if at all) on productivity tools. Productivity comes from the right mindset where you own your work: you have an agenda which has meaning and importance to you. Act like an owner, not a disempowered hired hand.

Chapter 5: 'Sell, sell, sell (without selling)'. In the past you could tell colleagues what to do. Now, you cannot tell; you have to sell. The more senior you are, the more you have to sell your ideas, priorities and agenda to have an impact. But no one likes to be a sales person and you should not be seen to sell. The riddle of selling without selling deepens with the discovery that decision making is not all rational: it is also deeply emotional and political. This chapter shows how you can manage rational, emotional and political decision making so that you can sell, without selling.

Decision making is not all rational

Chapter 6: 'Overcoming obstacles'. Opposition and obstacles are good news. They show that you are attempting to have real impact. If you want to have impact, you are going to upset people. Impact for you is about opportunity; for them it is about risk, more work, change and uncertainty. The greater your impact, the greater the obstacles you will face. This chapter shows how you can overcome obstacles, usually without the need to fight any corporate battles. At the heart of achieving this is the art of the hustle where you make it happen, change the reality on the ground and then ask for permission for what you have already done.

Chapter 7: 'Read the air: growing your formal power'. Previous chapters showed how you can use informal power to have impact far beyond the reach of your formal power and position. But gaining more formal power makes it easier to have even more impact. This chapter shows how you can gain more formal power through promotion. Discover how the rules of survival and success change at each level, and how promotion criteria change: early in your career technical skills and potential matter most; later in your career performance and managing people and politics matter most. You will also discover how to influence promotion decisions, which often do not follow the published HR process. This chapter makes visible the invisible rules of survival and success.

> **The rules of survival and success change at each level**

Chapter 8: 'Raise your inner game'. The best leaders are not always the most skilled. Their secret sauce is not their skill set: it is their mindset. They act differently because they think differently. Fortunately, mindset is just shorthand for habits of mind, which we can all learn if we want to. This chapter shows how you can acquire the seven plus one mindsets of success. It also shows how you can avoid the most common mindset traps which can trip you up.

Taken together, *Impact* shows how you can achieve more with less, or even no, power, authority, resources or budget. It shows you how organisations really work. You can make the organisation work for you once you understand how to manage rational, emotional and political decision making. *Impact* does not predict a revolution in management; it simply maps out the revolution in management that is happening in front of our noses. As with all revolutions, there will be winners and losers. *Impact* is your guide to doing more with less and to landing up on the right side of the revolution.

Why the challenge of impact is greater than ever: IQ, EQ and PQ

Management is becoming harder than ever. But it is also more rewarding than ever if you understand the new rules of survival and success. The skills you need to succeed have changed. Like many of the biggest changes, the changing skill set is not noticeable from day to day. But if you take a step back and look at the broader sweep of history, the change is dramatic.

Nineteenth century: IQ

In the 19th century, orders flowed downwards and information flowed back up. Everyone did as they were told. The job of the manager was to get ideas out of his (always his, in the 19th century) head, and into the hands of the workers. Thinking and doing were separate activities. The defining strength of management was IQ: you had to be smarter or more experienced than the people you managed.

Twentieth century: IQ and EQ

In the 20th century, workers did something revolutionary: they got educated. As a result, they could do more but they also expected more. They expected to be treated as humans, not as unreliable machines. This raised the bar for managers. It was no longer enough to be a brain on sticks. They had to learn the art of managing people: motivating them, delegating to them and even trusting them to make decisions and solve problems themselves. Managers had to build commitment, not just compliance. This new art of managing people became popularised as the era of EQ: emotional quotient.

Twenty-first century: IQ, EQ and PQ

In the 21st century, the bar has been raised again for managers. It is no longer enough to be smart (high IQ) and nice (high EQ). You can find plenty of nice and smart people who languish in relative obscurity, while people who are not so nice or smart forge ahead and make things happen. Something has changed.

Some of the changes in the 21st century are obvious: the rise of hybrid working and AI, and the reduction in discrimination in the workplace. But there is a deeper change as well. The new challenge is the challenge of control. Formal power is no longer enough. You need to acquire informal power to make things happen when you lack formal control.

The art of management has always involved the acquisition and use of power. In the past, formal power was all that managers needed. Now you need informal power to build the alliances, secure the support, find the resources, remove the obstacles and achieve the impact you want. This means that in addition to IQ and EQ, you also need PQ: political quotient.

Management has always involved the acquisition and use of power

PQ is how you build your informal power so that you can take control of your destiny and make more impact. Without PQ, you will work for the organisation, but the organisation will not work for you. *Impact* describes the PQ skill set you need in order to thrive in the new world order.

Doing more with less: how informal power amplifies your formal power

This combination of formal and informal power defines your ability to make things happen. Formal power is based on your:

- budget;
- team size;
- decision-making rights.

These sources of formal power flow from your position in the hierarchy: the more senior you are, the more positional power you have. Formal power and positional power are one and the same. But if you rely only on your formal power, you will underperform: you will not be able to make things happen in areas beyond your span of control.

In today's flatter organisations you need informal power which comes from four sources:

- *Referent power*: this is your personal power which you build by having a network of trusted allies across the firm who will support you and help you make things happen; it is the result of being the trusted colleague who gives as well as takes. And if you are trusted and valued by clients, you have an even stronger form of personal power because clients are the gateway to revenues and profit.

- *Agenda power*, where you control the agenda. You can acquire agenda power at any stage of your career by suggesting an idea or taking on an important task which others are avoiding because it is too difficult, or by starting something new.

- *Expertise*: everyone has to learn a craft skill such as coding, law, data analysis or teaching. This expertise is vital to ensure you are in demand early in your career. Later in your career your expert power becomes less important than your ability to make things happen through other people.

- *Information*: even if you are at the bottom of the mountain, you see things which are invisible to executives at the top of the mountain. You have perspectives, insight and knowledge which can help them and you.

This is a new world where you can build and use informal power from the start of your career. You can start having impact early: you do not need to wait for 20 years before reaching the mythical corner

office to start having impact. This
book shows how you can have
impact wherever you are in the
formal hierarchy.

**You can have impact
wherever you are in the
formal hierarchy**

Look at the figure below, and
you will recognise colleagues who fit each of the four types of formal
(positional) and informal (personal) power combinations.

	Low Personal power	High Personal power
High Positional power	Little dictators	Rainmakers
Low Positional power	Cogs in the machine	Hidden gems

Here is what the four types of colleagues look like in practice.

- *Rainmakers* have high formal and informal power. They use
  influence as much as authority to make things happen. Instead
  of telling people what to do and gaining compliance, they build
  commitment within and beyond the firm. Because people want
  to work with them, they attract the best teams and clients and
  achieve more as a result.

- *Little dictators* have formal authority, but do not even attempt
  to cultivate informal power. They are traditional managers who
  like processes, procedures, protocols and policies which they can
  enforce. Rules become a substitute for thinking or common sense.
  They can stop things happening, but they find it more or less
  impossible to build alliances which would allow them to make
  things happen beyond their own empire.

- *Cogs in the machine* have neither formal power nor informal
  power. All organisations depend on having many people like this

who can be relied on to do their job well. Often these are front line workers who enjoy working on the front line and have no desire to move into management roles which would take them away from what they like doing.

- *Hidden gems* have little formal power but magically make things happen because they have acquired great informal power. This book is about how you can acquire the magic to make things happen as a hidden gem and potential rainmaker.

Throughout this book you will discover real life cases from hidden gems: people with no formal power, no budget, no decision-making rights and no team making extraordinary things happen. This is an essential skill to acquire. No manager ever complains of having too much authority, budget and resource. It is usually the other way round. Your responsibilities normally exceed your authority and budget. Formal power is never enough to succeed. You have to acquire informal power: you need to learn the 21st century skill set of PQ, or political quotient. Do this well, and you will achieve more than anyone else thinks is possible.

About the book

Impact is the result of over 20 years' research on leadership. It started when I co-founded Teach First, which has become the largest graduate recruiter in the UK. As part of our offer to graduates, we included a leadership programme which we did not have and we could not afford. So I set out to develop one, which started by asking many eminent leaders of the day, 'what is leadership?' Their answers were all completely contradictory, so it is a question I have been attempting to answer ever since.

In that time, I have looked at leadership through every lens. I have interviewed and worked with thousands of executives around the world and in all industries; I have interviewed explorers, special forces, sportspeople and even been on the nuclear deterrent in search of the secret sauce of leadership. I have spent more time than is wise working with tribes and traditional societies around the world to see how they are led: they lead in the harshest of environments and without a safety net.

The result is that I have been able to map both the skill set and mindset of the most successful leaders. But as I was mapping the skill set and mindset, I realised that the reality on the ground was changing. The map that would have worked 20 years ago does not work today. There was a missing element. I could not understand how some people made great things happen, regardless of their position, while others did not make great things happen even if they were senior in their organisations.

The gap in theory was even more evident in practice: reality is always a good antidote to theory. In my work starting Teach First, starting a bank, building a business in Japan and helping start eight other NGOs, it was evident that the best leaders had a magic sauce which neither the literature nor the business schools picked up.

Eventually, I plucked up the courage to start asking some exceptional leaders a very dumb question: how do you really make things happen? Dumb questions are often good questions. Newton asked perhaps the dumbest question of all time: why do apples fall down, not shoot outwards or float upwards? That dumb question led to the discovery of gravity as a force which helped unravel the mysteries of the universe. My dumb question was humbler with a humbler result: it revealed PQ as the third force of management, in addition to IQ and EQ.

To ensure the answers were practical, I did not ask anyone for their opinions on how they make things happen. I asked them to describe in detail how they made (or failed to make) something big and difficult happen. I am hugely grateful to them for their honest answers, which populate this book. This book is not theory heavy: it is heavy on cases and practical experience from around the world.

The answers I received were consistent, which indicates that PQ is a real force which can be mapped, learned and applied by anyone. The consistency was surprising given the diversity of the people

I interviewed: from hospital porters to CEOs across the world and across industries and with an even gender balance. *Impact* does not predict a management revolution; it simply maps the revolution that is happening in front of our eyes.

The rules of survival and success are changing: *Impact* is your guide to the new rules and how you can use them to achieve even more, wherever you are in your career.

chapter 1

Become the colleague of choice

Discover how to amplify your formal power and impact by making things happen through people you do not control: become the partner that colleagues want to help and support. This is a curious world where givers achieve more than takers: you achieve more by being generous, selfless, helping others and supporting their agenda as well as yours. Welcome to the world of influence and trust.

If you want to have real impact you cannot do it all yourself. The lone hero saving the world exists only in the movies. You have to make things happen with other people. In the past, you made things happen through

You have to make things happen through people you do not control

people you controlled. Now you have to make things happen through people you do not control.

You need the support of other departments who are competing with you for that limited pot of top leadership support, budget and bonuses; you may have to work with suppliers, customers and other external stakeholders. If all of these people want to work with you, you will have created a super power which enables you to have impact far beyond your formal authority. Informal power massively amplifies your formal power.

To have impact and do more with less, you have to invest in yourself. Make yourself the partner of choice for colleagues, bosses, suppliers and customers. When you weave your web of influence across and beyond your organisation, you free yourself from the tyranny of hierarchy. You are no longer constrained by your budget, decision-making rights and span of control. Instead, they become the platform from which you can build your informal power. By combining your formal power with informal power, you can have more impact. You can do far more with far less.

Understanding how to build trust and build your informal power will help you whatever you do, wherever you are. It may even help you borrow camels from royalty when you need them. Knowing how to borrow camels from royalty may or may not be a vital skill in your firm, but the skills you need to achieve this are universal.

The great camel challenge was acute for Mark Evans, the founder of Outward Bound's highly successful Oman branch. He decided to lead an expedition across the infamous Empty Quarter of Arabia, from Oman to Qatar. Because of security and safety concerns, he needed the blessing of three governments. He also needed camels in a hurry: the camels which he had been promised had not materialised. There is only a small time window in winter when it is possible to cross the Empty Quarter. This is the stuff of nightmares for any manager: your big project is kicking off with high visibility from top management, and you get derailed at the last moment. You need to find a solution, fast.

Mark Evans's solution was simple and dramatic. He asked the Omani Royal Cavalry if they could lend four of their camels for the expedition. They did so immediately because the Sultan of Oman wanted the expedition to go ahead. At the border, they were met by the Saudis who provided an escort across the desert. At the next border, with Qatar, they were expedited past the border controls to be met by another set of camels which the Emir of Qatar kindly offered Mark and his team. So why would Saudi Arabia, Qatar and Oman go out of their way to help Mark's expedition?

Their support was the result of many years of building trust and building relationships with each government:

- Oman: Mark founded Outward Bound in Oman. He turned it into a force for helping younger Omanis, and for building connections across cultures. The Duke of Edinburgh was a patron of Outward Bound for many years and helped make connections in the early years, which Mark built up by proving that he was a credible partner and good friend of all things Omani.

- Qatar: Mark recognised that Qatar deeply values its heritage. He visited the Middle East Centre at Oxford University and found pictures of the original Bertram Thomas expedition across the Empty Quarter in 1931. These included pictures of Qatar as it was, and the Emir's ancestors. The expedition became a way of highlighting and celebrating Qatar's heritage.

- Saudi Arabia wanted to improve relations with both Oman and Qatar, and this was a modest way of improving co-operation. A letter from Prince (now King) Charles helped pave the way.

All of this only happened because Mark spent many years building relationships, building trust and building influence. He displayed three core elements of building trust and influence which you can use at work, even when you are not in urgent need of borrowing some camels:

- *Find a common goal*: Mark worked hard to understand the very different agendas of Oman, Qatar and Saudi Arabia. He was then able to show how his expedition would support them and their needs. He focused on their needs, not his.

- *Build credibility*: many years of developing Outward Bound in Oman showed that Mark could be trusted to deliver. His track record of leading expeditions across deserts and the Arctic showed that he could also lead a successful expedition.

- *Be selfless*: Mark is always generous with his time and generous in his spirit. He is one of the world's givers, not takers. This makes it easy to trust him and work with him: you know that something good will happen and he is not in it for himself.

An old-style manager could never have done what Mark Evans did. Command and control might have worked in the era of the Empire when you could lead expeditions wherever you wanted to; it does not work today where you need the support of different governments. As a private citizen you cannot control three foreign governments. You have to make things happen through people and organisations you do not control. You have to be the colleague people want to work with, not the colleague they have to work with.

Even within your own team, you cannot rely on command and control. If you manage professionals, you manage people who do not want to be controlled. Professionals take pride in their jobs and do not want, or need, to be micromanaged. They expect to be trusted. A short conversation around the coffee machine normally reveals what professionals really think: they think that management is largely a waste of space, and that they could do your job better than you can.

The good news about managing professionals is that they can do far more than the semi-educated masses of the past. The bad news is that they resent being controlled. If you want to unleash their potential, you have to become the manager of choice, not the manager they have to work with because of the vagaries of the assignment system. If you are the manager of choice, you will be able to recruit the best talent to your team. You will have far more impact with the 'A' team than if you have to work with the 'B' team.

To make things happen in this new world, you need old-world formal power and you need new-world informal power. Informal power is your force multiplier which allows you to do more with less.

At the heart of your informal power is becoming the colleague of choice and the manager of choice. So how do

Informal power is your force multiplier which allows you to do more with less

you become the colleague and manager that everyone wants to work with and wants to help? How do you make your power work for you, and how do you amplify your power?

The effective use of power is an age-old question. Over 500 years ago, Machiavelli wrote *The Prince* as a guide to being an effective ruler. In the book he asks a fundamental question which you might try to answer: is it better for the prince (or manager) to be feared or loved?

Machiavelli's conclusion is that it is better to be feared, because love is fickle. Here is what he wrote about the perils of popularity:

> **For this can be said of men in general: that they are ungrateful, fickle, hypocrites and dissemblers, avoiders of dangers, greedy for gain; and while you benefit them, they are entirely yours, offering you their blood, their goods, their life, their children, . . . when need is far away, but when you actually become needy, they turn away.**

You can decide whether human nature has changed in the last 500 years or not. But whatever you think of people today, Machiavelli was right to warn of the dangers of trying to be popular as a leader. Keeping a bowl of candy by your desk will make you popular for as long as the candy lasts; although you may be popular, people may not want to work with you. If you are a leader who craves popularity, you will avoid the difficult conversations and decisions; you will accept all the excuses about why a deadline needs to be moved back, or a budget might not be met. When you accept excuses, you accept failure. Popularity is the high road to weakness.

> **When you accept excuses, you accept failure. Popularity is the high road to weakness**

If popularity is the wrong road to take, what about fear? Machiavelli recommended a few executions to keep the population in order. Top managers may no longer execute their colleagues, but they will often undertake a restructuring which moves power barons, opponents and incompetents out of the firm. That is a career execution and it is an effective way of securing your formal power.

The problem with fear-based leadership is that no one will want to work with you. You can be an old-school tyrant with your own team, but you will find it hard to recruit the best team. Fear will not convince colleagues in other departments to go out of their way for you. To have real impact, you need colleagues who will put in that little bit of extra effort for you: they will warn you of problems, find new solutions to you, give you early warning of new opportunities and they will prioritise helping you over helping all the other colleagues who are also demanding a slice of their time.

When Machiavelli asked whether it is better to be feared or loved, the best answer is 'neither'. The true currency of informal power is neither fear nor love: it is trust. As a trusted colleague you earn respect and build influence; you will find ways of having difficult conversations positively; you will stick to your budget and goals and you will make things happen.

Trust is a small word with a big meaning. As a manager, trust is built on five pillars, with a quick reminder of how Mark Evans deployed them to great effect:

- *Social alignment.* We find it easier to deal with people who are like ourselves. We understand what they really mean when they talk, and we understand what they don't say. We have shared experiences to draw on. This is good for efficiency and ease of communication, not so good for diversity. Mark was not just respectful of local culture, he absorbed it and became an authority on some aspects of local history. He was an outsider who was accepted on the inside.

- *Goal alignment.* Members of a team with a common goal work for each other and look after each other: self-interest and common interest walk hand in hand. It is hard to trust someone who has a competing agenda with yours. Finding common ground between your agenda and theirs is hard: when you achieve it, you are able to work together. Mark did not just pitch his needs to each government: he understood their needs and showed how the expedition could help them. He aligned his needs with theirs.

> **It is hard to trust someone who has a competing agenda with yours**

- *Credibility,* which is about doing as you say. 'Doing' is relatively easy for professionals who take pride in their job and want to deliver. The problem is normally in the 'saying'. What we say and what others hear are often very different. The resulting mismatch of expectations is the source of constant conflict and tension. The 'I said you said she meant but he didn't and they could have but we never. . .' discussion after the event simply makes matters worse. Over 20 years of building Outward Bound in Oman showed that Mark would do as he says; his history of completed expeditions showed that he could cross the Empty Quarter successfully.

- *Selflessness.* We all have colleagues who are in it for themselves. They are often toxic on teams, even if they perform well. These takers thrive in traditional hierarchies but struggle where you need co-operation. Givers, not takers, will rule in the new world of work. Givers have ambition for the mission, not for themselves. Mark focused on the mission, not himself.

> **Givers have ambition for the mission, not for themselves**

- *Risk*. The riskier the situation, the more trust I need. I may trust a stranger to give me directions to a shop; I would be unwise to trust a random stranger with my wallet, cards and phone. Smart managers learn to tilt the change equation in their favour: make it easy to support you, but risky to oppose you. With Mark's expedition, none of the three governments wanted the bad publicity of stopping a venture backed by two other governments.

We can combine these five elements into a trust equation as follows:

$$t = (Sa \times G \times C \times S) / R$$

The maths may be spurious, but the meaning is clear: you will become the trusted colleague and partner if you: build social alignment (Sa), find goal alignment with your peers (G), you earn credibility by doing as you say (C) and you are seen to be selfless (S). As we shall see, you have to manage risk (R) appropriately as well.

Trust is the basic building block of your informal power. Achieving impact also requires you to weave your web of influence, build the right alliances, work on the right agenda, sell your ideas, navigate the politics of the firm and deal with the inevitable crises and opportunities that work throws up. Doing these things becomes far harder if you are not trusted. You may have to work with colleagues you do not trust from time to time, but do you ever want to work with such people?

This chapter will show how you can put the five pillars of trust in place and become the colleague of choice. Subsequent chapters will show how you can use trust to have a bigger impact and do more with less.

Build social alignment

A team with different perspectives, skills and values is more effective than a team of clones. The diverse team may be more effective, but it is also much harder to make it work because team members will not understand each other so easily. It is easier to understand people who have a shared background, experiences and values. Conformity makes work easy; diversity makes work more effective.

> **Conformity makes work easy; diversity makes work more effective**

If you want to be the team member or manager that people want to work with, you have to find alignment with people who are not like you. Fortunately, there is a magic potion which will miraculously help you win friends and influence people, especially if you drink it slowly. The potion is called 'coffee' or sometimes 'tea' and is widely available. The way to administer this potion is to sit down with whoever you want to influence, drink the potion slowly while talking about nothing in particular. If in doubt, ask the person to talk about their favourite subject: themselves.

There is one more trick you have to master in weaving your magic. For this, you need the key attribute of all the best leaders, managers and sales people. You need to have two ears and one mouth. And you need to use them in that proportion. The easiest way to win friends is to listen to them. In a time-starved world, listening is a strong form of flattery. It shows that you value the other person enough that you

> **The easiest way to win friends is to listen to them**

want to invest your time in hearing their story. Invariably, they will think that you have very fine judgement because you want to listen to them.

At this point, you may ask, 'Why should I waste my time on idle chitchat when there is important work to be done and urgent deadlines to be met? How can I make an impact and do more with less if I am just chatting all the time?'

The simplest response came from Tarek Alami, when he was running the Middle East operations of EDT, which is in the education business: 'Why should I want to work with someone I do not trust?' This is a view which echoes around the world. Here is Sally

Maier-Yip, founder and managing director of 11K Consulting talking about doing business in China:

> **The client wants to know you as a person before they do business with you. So I always buy lunch first where we talk about non-business matters such as families and holidays. In China and with Chinese people, we always do business over lunch. Lunch is where you do the bonding and at the end they may say send me a proposal once the trust is built.**

Building trust with external stakeholders is obvious, but it is equally important to build trust with colleagues inside your organisation. Even in Japan, the hard-working 'salaryman' is expected to attend *nomikai*, an after-work drinking party where colleagues can put the world to rights.

In the West, we often assume that trust comes pre-packaged with the brand name of your employer and your qualifications. But having an MBA from Harvard and working for a top investment bank does not make you instantly trustworthy. In practice, you have to invest time in building trust and relationships wherever you are in the world. The existence of the global corporate entertainment business illustrates the value firms place on building social connections across and within firms.

The power of this approach became clear when a senior Google executive flew to Paris to meet her European team, before flying on to London. The meeting was required because there had been too much miscommunication and mistrust across the Atlantic. The clear-the-air meeting was packed with all the issues which needed to be addressed. It did not go well: although they found a way forward on most issues, it was clear that there was still mistrust. The meeting had addressed the symptoms, not the causes, of the mistrust and miscommunication.

The executive's day proceeded to get worse: her flight to London was cancelled because of an air traffic controllers' strike. This meant she had to take the train, along with some other colleagues who had been in the meeting with her. She described what happened next:

It was like a miracle. When we got on the train at Gare du Nord, we did not really know each other or trust each other. Three hours later we got off at St Pancras, and we felt we all knew each other properly. As a result, the quality of communication improved dramatically for the next year. For the first time, we were a real team.

Even at Google, high touch beats high tech. Meeting people in person matters: that is where you can build the human contact and start to understand each other. This matters in the world of hybrid work, where we have discovered that we communicate more than ever but understand each other as little as ever. Remote communication is very effective for transactional work, especially where team members already know and trust each other. Remote communication is less effective for building trust and personal relationships.

> **High touch beats high tech**

> **We communicate more than ever but understand each other as little as ever**

If you are working remotely, it is harder, but not impossible, to build social alignment. A simple hack is to curate your video background. This is your chance to disclose what you want to disclose about yourself. Professional qualifications, pictures of holidays, family or hobbies, or interesting objects all give your colleagues a chance to ask a question and start a conversation. Choose your background to reveal something about yourself and let your colleagues get to know you personally.

Making the effort to meet in person can be transformational. Kat Narayanan was head of Salesforce's South Asian Equality Group. This was a 100 per cent voluntary role which involved working with people around the globe, often on sensitive issues. She had a simple way of building the necessary bonds of trust: she took time off to meet people in person. Here is her story:

> **So when I went to Dublin on a personal trip I made a point of calling in on the Dublin office to meet some people there. Just recently I went to Amsterdam on a holiday and I left my friends for an afternoon and I went into the Amsterdam office on my personal time to say hello to some colleagues who I had not met in person before. I met two or three colleagues for about 30 minutes each. We probably only spoke about our work for 10 minutes. But in that time, we broke down barriers and we built trust and the quality of communication has improved greatly as a result.**
>
> **You should treat everyone with the same courtesy and respect. Invest in every potential relationship. You might not appreciate the impact of that meeting at that time but the fruits of your efforts will always appear in the most unexpected moments in the future.**

Taking time out of your holiday to meet colleagues socially is a serious investment of time, and one which colleagues will remember vividly. If you think of chitchat as wasting time, you will not do it. If you think of it as investing time to build trust and be more effective, you will make the effort.

The simple act of listening represents a cultural revolution in more traditional firms. Low listening firms focus on immediate results, not on the people or the process: they are led by 'what', not 'how', which results in a more competitive and less collaborative culture which works in silos. Marco Maccari, a senior HR professional in Italy, put it simply:

> **For me soft power is all about listening. You put the people first and then you get the results.**

The key to doing more with less is not to work longer and harder. The key is to work through other people: harness their abilities and talents to help you meet your important goal and urgent deadline. Why should they want to work with you if they do not trust you?

Social alignment is not a waste of time. It is an investment of time which will keep paying you dividends in the form of increased trust, better communication and more support for what you do and what you need.

Build credibility

Building social alignment is a good start, but it is not enough to build trust. We all have friends we like greatly, but we would probably not rely on them unless we had no other choice. Your next vital step in becoming the trusted partner of colleagues is to build your credibility.

Most professionals feel slightly offended when asked to build credibility, because most professionals take pride in what they do and believe that they are already credible. Credibility is in the eye of the beholder. You may know that you are credible and reliable, but if you are a new team member no one else will know that. You have to earn your credibility. Building credibility involves three challenges:

Credibility is in the eye of the beholder

1 Doing as you say.

2 Achieving 100 per cent consistency.

3 Finding credibility at speed when the stakes are high.

These challenges matter because credibility is like a vase: it takes time to craft and a moment to destroy. Once you lose credibility, it is like trying to repair a broken vase: it takes great effort and is never really the same again. If you are liked but not credible, you will be popular in the office but you will not be effective.

Here are the three credibility challenges:

1 *Doing as you say.* How hard is this? Any self-respecting professional will believe that they do as they say. They will also recount the many times that they have been let down by colleagues who

We judge ourselves by our intentions and others by their actions

are also professionals. We judge ourselves more kindly than we judge others. This is because we judge ourselves by our intentions and others by their actions. We know that we are doing our best and we have good intentions. But your colleagues are not mind readers. They do not know your intentions. All they can see are your actions, so they judge you by your actions.

This gap between saying and doing is the cause of endless conflict and argument within and across teams. The problem is that what we say and what is heard is often very different. When a colleague asks for some help you might say something like 'I will look into it. . . I will do my best. . . I will see what is possible'. You are clearly not promising to make something happen. But what is heard may well be 'I will do it'. Two weeks later you may come back and honestly report that you did your best and looked into it, but nothing was possible. At that point, all credibility has been lost and the 'I said you said and she didn't and you could have but we never. . . ' debate simply makes things worse.

Professionals like to be liked, which is why they always make an effort to deliver. This makes them weak on 'saying' because they do not want to cause offence or let colleagues down. If you want to maintain credibility, it is better to have a difficult conversation about expectations at the outset, than an impossible conversation about outcomes after the event.

2 *Achieving 100 per cent consistency,* which is the essence of the quality movement: you want the one millionth computer chip to be exactly the same as all the others. If someone lets you down once, you will remember that far more vividly than all the other times they quietly delivered for you. This extends from the largest commitments to the smallest. If you cannot be trusted on small commitments, you will not be trusted on larger commitments. Here is Kat Narayanan again:

If I bump into someone in reception and they ask me to make an introduction to someone else in the company, despite not interacting with them for very

long I'll always make sure to follow through with a promise. . . . And if around the water cooler someone says they're going to Amsterdam I make recommendations about what they can do. . . . I always follow up even on personal commitments and even on the smallest thing.

3 *Finding credibility at speed when the stakes are high.* Building credibility takes time because you need to build a track record. You know about your qualifications and impressive achievements, but very often your partners will not know this. If you are presenting to senior executives for the first time, or you are selling to a new customer, or trying to influence a regulator, they will have little idea about your track record and whether you are credible or not. At this point you need to find a way of establishing credibility at speed: you need a credibility hack.

The easiest way to establish credibility at speed is to borrow it. A few examples will make the point:

When I started Teach First, which is now the largest graduate recruiter in the UK, we had more or less nothing. We had no money, no team and no educational experience. So why would anyone want to talk to us? The only thing we had was the use of some offices, kindly provided by McKinsey. That gave us immediate credibility. Although we were complete unknowns to the educational establishment, we were able to invite people to meet us in the McKinsey offices. As soon as we met one power broker, we referenced that in our next conversation. Blagging like that gets you the meeting: after that you have to prove you can do as you say.

Just as places give you credibility, so do people. Sharath Jeevan, founding CEO of STIR Education, was in Karnataka, India, for a few days and needed to speak with the education minister, who he did not know. He convinced the minister to give him ten minutes of his time on a very busy day. He used those ten minutes wisely. He established a common goal and need around education. He then flattered the minister by saying how highly he had been talked of at a ministerial meeting which Sharath had attended the previous week. This established Sharath's credibility by showing he moved in similar circles to the minister: they were peers.

Borrowing credibility works within your firm as well. If you are putting a proposal to top management, one of the first questions they will be asking themselves is, 'do I believe this proposal?' If they have not heard of you, you can expect that they will read the proposal very critically and you will need to be ready for plenty of challenge. You can borrow the credibility you need by getting buy-in, in private, from key executives before presenting your report. The key is to ask each executive to validate just the one part of your proposal which relates to their area of expertise. Ask the marketing people to validate your marketing ideas, ask the IT people to validate the technical viability of your idea. Don't give each executive a veto over your proposal by letting them comment on the whole package, including areas where they are not expert. The Japanese have a name for this slow process of consensus building: *nemawashi*. Let people disagree in private, but agree in public. Never use a meeting for a decision; only use it to confirm in public the agreements you have reached in private. By the time your proposal arrives at the meeting, its credibility will be beyond doubt because it has the backing of all the most credible people in the room.

> **Never use a meeting for a decision**

Goal alignment

If you have ever played on a sports team, you will know what it is like to chase a common goal. There is a sense of camaraderie that comes from everyone being dependent on everyone else. You cannot succeed unless they succeed, and they cannot succeed unless you succeed. This mutual dependence creates a sense of common purpose and common commitment. Peer group pressure brings out the best in everyone. No one wants to be the person that let the side down. Aligning goals

> **Peer group pressure brings out the best in everyone**

is a powerful way to build trust and achieve far greater impact than any one person can achieve.

Equally, you have probably been in situations where you doubt the other person has your best interests at heart. A second-hand car salesperson may well want to help you, but the nagging suspicion is that they just want to offload a piece of junk on you for top dollar, confident that they will never have to see you again. Lack of trust is more or less built into such high-value, one-off transactions.

Within your firm, in theory, everyone should have aligned goals. In the private sector, that normally comes in the form of focus on profit and making this quarter's budget. In practice, firms are set up for conflict. This comes as a surprise to management theorists, but no surprise to anyone who actually works in a firm. So, for the speed readers, it is worth repeating the point: firms are set up for conflict.

Every department and business unit is competing for the same limited pot of management time, support and budget. Even within the team, there is competition for the next promotion, for the best assignment and the best bonus: not everyone will be a winner. You compete with the colleagues you work with.

Your challenge is to make sure that your goals and your agenda receive the support they need to succeed. All your peers are trying to make sure that their goals and agenda receive the support they need. Welcome to the tournament.

Starting Teach First: the wrong way and the right way

Teach First is now the largest graduate recruiter in the UK and has recruited over 18,000 teachers into the profession. It very nearly died before it was born.

Over six months we worked hard to build a bulletproof case to prove to the government that they should fund this new way of recruiting and training teachers. We did everything right.

➤

We overcame all the objections: how would the teachers be trained, how much should they be paid, will the unions object, will any graduates actually want to join and teach in areas of disadvantage? We had answers for everything. We went to the final meeting with the minister, which was a chance for him to give his seal of approval to our idea.

The minister arrived slightly late, looked embarrassed and said: 'Thank you for putting in so much effort on this, but we have decided that on balance it is just too risky.' He then left at speed and we were left wondering what had gone wrong.

We could not understand why the minister thought the programme would fail. So we prepared an even more robust business case to show that the idea was 100 per cent guaranteed to succeed. While doing this, I quietly talked to civil servants to find out why the minister thought it was so risky. The real risk was that if Teach First succeeded, that would show that the minister's own programme for teacher recruitment was a failure. He had to kill Teach First, not because it might fail but because it might succeed and embarrass him. Only in government will ideas get killed because they might succeed.

We changed course. If we went back 'proving' that we would succeed, we would be rejected even more forcefully. So we went back and showed that our idea was very modest, it would sit alongside and not duplicate or compete with existing programmes. The minister started purring like a cat and the idea was approved.

Two years later, Teach First replaced the minister's pet project. But by that time, we ensured that Teach First had become 'his' idea. Our goal had become his goal: goal alignment matters.

Goal alignment is not about persuading people that you are right. The typical way that smart people think is shown in Figure 1.1.

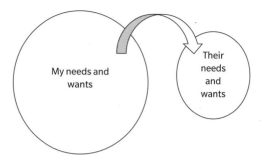

Figure 1.1 The ineffective persuasive mindset

The traditional mindset tries to get the ideas out of your head and into the head of the other person. This rarely works, much to the frustration of smart colleagues. A common refrain I hear from executives and consultants goes like this: 'I can't believe they were so dumb. I made a bulletproof case. It was so clear, so obvious. Why can't they get it?'

Trying to persuade people that you are right may be intellectually and morally satisfying, but it is not effective. How often do you hear people put their hand up and say: 'OK, you have persuaded me. You are right and I am wrong?' No one likes to be proven wrong, ever. Persuasion is not just about logic: it is about emotion and politics:

- *Emotion*: I don't want to look stupid, to be proven wrong in public, to embarrass myself by changing my position in public; I want to be respected and valued.

- *Politics*: how will this decision affect me, my department and my career: will it lead to opportunities or problems, to more or less work, to conflict with other departments?

Your rational case does not even begin to touch the emotional and political sides of a decision. This is where things go wrong. You may have a bulletproof case, but if it is an idea which is going to cause problems for your colleague, they will find all sorts of reasons to oppose your idea. You will then argue your rational case even harder, to which you will get further objections which appear to be increasingly irrational. The problem is not the logic of your case.

The real problem is emotional and political: these are problems which are invisible to you. Fighting emotion with reason is like fighting fire with fuel: exciting for observers to watch, but dangerous and wholly counterproductive.

> **Fighting emotion with reason is like fighting fire with fuel**

Your idea may be very important to you, but it is likely to be less important than dog food to your colleague. If they ignore your idea, not much will happen. If they ignore the dog's food, the dog will let them know in no uncertain terms. Your project may be vital to you, but for the finance department which has to vet your figures it is not important: you are simply one of many executives who wants their time and support in approving your business case. Why should they put you at the front of the queue and give you special, favourable treatment?

This is where you need to start a mental revolution. Instead of seeing the world through your eyes, see the world through their eyes. You need to give at least as much prominence to their needs and wants as to yours. This does not mean slavishly giving them everything they want and abandoning your needs and wants. Instead, you have to find a middle ground where your needs meet their needs (Figure 1.2). In the case of Teach First (above) there was a rational need to place more excellent teachers into areas of

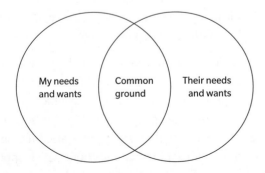

Figure 1.2 The effective and influential mindset

disadvantage. But that was not the minister's need. The minister's need was to be seen as a successful Secretary of State for Education. We had to show how Teach First would not threaten him, and could enhance his legacy.

Finding common ground is easier said than done. But this is where you deploy the key skill highlighted in the last section, on credibility: listening. If you do all the talking, you will never find out what is motivating your colleague. If you listen well, you will discover all you need to make your case.

Listening does not start at the moment you need to make your pitch. It starts long before. For instance, if you want to propose a big business case to the board, you know you will need sign off from the finance department beforehand. It is no use going to them a few days before the board meeting and trying to hustle them into approval. Even before you start building your business case, go to the finance department and ask for their advice. Officials are wary of giving approval, but are delighted to give advice: that shows they are being respected and valued. The sort of advice you need from the finance department may include the following:

- What criteria will they use for evaluating this case?

- What evidence and data will they need to see?

- Who should you work with in the department to help build the case?

- When do they need to see the final case? What does their workload look like and can you do anything to make it easier?

- What other initiatives do you need to be aware of, are there any obstacles which might derail this case?

You can take the same approach to every department which has to vet and approve your idea. By involving them at the earliest stage, they become your partners, not your opponents. Do this well and you will not even need to persuade them when you produce the final business case: they will be your advocates. You will not need to win the argument, because you will already have won a friend.

This influential mindset does not require world-class persuasion skills. It requires world-class listening skills. Great listening is not about keeping quiet until you can jump in and make your point. Great listening is about understanding, and showing that you understand. There is a simple technique you can use to achieve this: paraphrasing.

> **This influential mindset does not require world-class persuasion skills. It requires world-class listening skills**

When a colleague makes a point to you, it is tempting to make your own point back in return: you might agree or disagree, but you make your point. By making your point you may prove to yourself that you are smart, but you prove nothing to your colleague. In particular, you do not prove that your colleague has been heard or understood. It is very frustrating when someone appears not to hear you or understand you.

How not to persuade

We finally got a meeting with the prisons minister. We wanted his support for a programme which reduced re-offending by more than 90 per cent. The rational case was bulletproof, because it was backed by real-world experience.

The CEO had spent many years fighting a prisons system which did not care about rehabilitation. She was rightly angry about government policy, which led to so many prisoners re-offending within a year of release from prison. Many would re-offend the day they left prison by going straight to their nearest drugs dealer.

We agreed that this was not the time to tell the minister where he was going wrong. It was time to listen, make a friend and gain his support for our programme. After five minutes of listening to the minister's waffle, the CEO could take no more. She let fly and told him exactly what she thought of his

---

government. She was very pleased that she had finally been
able to make her point to the minister directly.

The meeting ended five minutes later, we gained no support
and the programme eventually folded as a result.

Telling people is rarely persuasive. If you want to persuade,
listen. You have two ears and one mouth: use them in that
proportion.

Instead of making your point, paraphrase back to your colleague,
in your own words, what you think she said. A typical paraphrasing
reply might start with, 'So what you are telling me is. . . so the key
issue you have identified is. . . so what you want is. . . '. This simple
trick is powerful because:

- you show you have understood your colleague;

- your colleague no longer feels the need to keep repeating their
  point because they fear that have not been heard or understood.
  They are more likely to shut up and be ready to listen to you;

- your colleague feels respected and valued: you start to win a
  friend;

- if there is a misunderstanding, you quickly find it and can fix it;

- you are not agreeing or disagreeing: you are only showing that
  you understand them;

- you avoid unnecessary conflict or confusion.

All of this takes time, but it is a case of going slow to speed up. Time
pressure is your enemy. Do not feel you have to rush in and make
your point and prove your case. Rushing in will slow you down
because you will find yourself having to deal with all sorts of unexpected questions and objections which will appear rational, but may
be hiding emotional and political objections.

Take time early to exercise your world-class listening skills, when
you are not in a rush. This is when you quietly build buy-in and support for your idea. You uncover their agendas; you find the common
ground and you become partners, not adversaries. By the time you

reach the deadline and everything is becoming a last-minute rush, you will find that all your key stakeholders are ready to say yes. The last-minute rush becomes a gentle stroll for you.

The influential mindset has a different way of thinking from the persuasive mindset:

- Focus on their needs and wants, not just yours.
- Find the win/win in the common ground; avoid win/lose arguments.
- Listen more than you speak, to discover their needs and wants.
- Ask smart questions instead of giving smart answers.
- Collaborate, don't compete.
- Win a friend, not an argument.

> **Win a friend, not an argument**

Be selfless

In my research with over 1,000 leaders, I always ask them what they really want from their team members. To my surprise, one of the top five attributes they expect from a team member is ambition. At first, this sounds like they want pushy types who are always 'me, me, me'. In the old world of command and control, that may have worked. You had to be personally ambitious and competitive to gain each promotion and to gain more formal power. That was a recipe for politics and conflict, so why would leaders want ambition from team members today?

It turns out that there are two sorts of ambition: 'me, me, me' and 'we, we, we'. The ambition that leaders want today is around ambition for the mission and an ambition to make a difference. Team members who are ambitious for the mission and for the team will find innovative ways of working, they will step up to help on new initiatives, they will go the extra mile to make things happen. They are outstanding team members.

Ambition for self versus ambition for the team transforms you from being a painful team member to being an ideal team member. Selflessness is not weak; it is a way to build trust and become the colleague of choice.

At work you probably know people who are always in it for themselves. They may or may not be good performers, but they are rarely the sort of colleagues you want to work with. And if colleagues don't want to work with you, why would external partners want to work with you? When success depends on making things happen through people you do not control, you have to be trusted. Being selfless turns out to be a very good way of taking by giving: generosity pays for itself.

Here are three ways you can be selfless, and you can give to take:

- Give your time.
- Put your partners' agenda first.
- Give away all the credit for success.

We will briefly look at each of these in turn.

Give your time

Think of the bosses and colleagues that you have most valued working with. Are they the ones that ignored you and rarely had any time for you, beyond the formal interactions of reviews, assessments and reports? Or are they the ones that always seemed to find time to listen to you and advise you, even if the advice was occasionally a little uncomfortable?

Once again, listening turns out to be a hidden super power that enables you to become the colleague of choice. By listening you show you value your colleague or team member; you respect their opinions. You also discover their needs and wants and what really motivates them.

If you give some time to your colleagues to help them out, they will feel the need to reciprocate. You win an ally and win future support. Some colleagues are selfish and will always take and never give back: you can join all your more generous colleagues in dialling down your support for selfish colleagues who will find themselves isolated.

Senior managers always need help to develop new ideas, look into opportunities or issues or just be an extra pair of hands. Volunteering to help out is a great way to cultivate a potential sponsor, gain visibility and to position yourself for an attractive assignment. Giving is a good way of taking.

Giving is a good way of taking

Put your partners' agenda first

This is difficult, but powerful. It is difficult because you are under constant pressure to perform, so putting someone else's needs first seems like an act of madness. It was a challenge Tarek Alami faced when he inherited a client project which was going awry in the Middle East: it was overspending and underdelivering. Inevitably he faced pressure from the finance department to just finish the project, deliver the margin and get out. But Tarek knew that the client was important. He wanted to build a long-term relationship rather than have a short-term transaction. A profitable transaction today would forfeit the long-term potential of the client.

Tarek pushed back: instead of putting financial results first, he put the client's interests first. In his words:

The first thing I said to our partners was that I have no interest in the follow-on contract so let's just get that out of the way. Instead, my focus was on how we could complete the existing contract properly so that we could close it and say goodbye on good terms. I did not want discussions about the new contract to get between us and to stop us sorting out the problems on the existing contract. You cannot talk about the future unless you have fixed the past. In this way we were able to create a productive working partnership.

This approach required strength in resisting the demands for short-term results from head office. But it meant that he regained the trust of the client, who then quietly confessed that many of the contract problems had been their responsibility. When the contract came to a successful conclusion, there was no need for further discussion: the follow-on contract came naturally. As Tarek noted, the contract was not just about results; it was about how they worked together.

Give away all the credit for success

You have just engineered an outstanding success. Why would you choose to give away all the credit to everyone else? Isn't this the time to blow your own trumpet and ensure that everyone recognises what a great job you have done? There are two reasons you should do this:

- You win friends and allies.
- You gain double the credit for your success.

You win friends and allies. We live in a praise-starved world. The success of social media shows how much we crave approval from our peers. Each 'like' on our social media feed is another addictive dopamine hit. At work, those dopamine hits are hard to find: 'thank you' is a simple word which is greatly underused. A very easy way to win friends and allies is to thank people more often. An even better and bigger dopamine hit is to praise them in public. Even if you think their contribution was small, they will think their contribution was big. This is your chance to go large and go public with the praise: pile on the appreciation and pile on the dopamine. The person you are praising will discover that you have very fine judgement, and will want to reciprocate your kindness in due course. You have won a new friend and ally.

You gain double the credit for your success. By praising everyone who helped with your big success you demonstrate that you were the person at the centre of the success: who else would be qualified to know who to praise and what to praise them for? Instead of arguing about who should gain all the credit, you have taken the credit by giving it away. Giving away the credit doubles your credit because you will be seen to be generous and a great team player or manager.

Giving away the credit doubles your credit

This selflessness is a good way to build your network from an early stage in your career. In any organisation you need a network of trusted allies. This is particularly obvious in complex global organisations like the OECD, the United Nations and the Commonwealth, where Steve Cutts has been a chef de cabinet and an assistant general secretary. He talks about always giving away the credit, at every stage of his career. In the early days this was about 'building a reservoir of support and goodwill' which is vital in highly political organisations where you have to build consensus among many different nations and viewpoints. At senior levels, selflessness remained the key to effectiveness: 'You have to let the politicians and other people get the credit for any big agreement. You will be far more successful if you let someone else take the credit because otherwise these powerful people will block you.' You may have been the sherpa that did all the hard work, but never take the spotlight away from your boss.

In the short term, claiming all the credit is a good tactic to boost yourself. In the long term, it is a lousy strategy which deters colleagues from helping you and makes you look selfish. Giving away the credit is an effective strategy: you take more by giving more.

The fifth element: risk

Risk presents a paradox. To have impact, you have to take risks: to try new things, to change things, to challenge things. But most managers are risk averse, and become more risk averse with seniority. At junior levels, the stakes are low and mistakes are easily forgiven. At senior levels, you have to make your numbers which makes it harder to take risks.

The obvious way to manage risk is to reduce it. This is what all those risk logs with their RAG (or BRAG) ratings and mitigating actions are all about. But they only deal with rational risks, such as an IT outage. It does not deal with emotional and political risks which ask, 'How will this idea affect me, my work and my position?'

Later chapters will show how you can identify the real risks, not just the rational risks, and how you can deal with them. For now, it is sufficient to note that there is an alternative way of managing risk, which is to increase it.

Why would anyone want to increase the perceived risk, when risk is like kryptonite to trust?

The reason is that risk is relative. **Risk is relative**

For instance, if I invited you to spend a night in an open boat among icebergs in the middle of the Atlantic you might choose to decline my risky offer. But if you were on the *Titanic* on 14 April 1912, you would have seen very grand first-class ladies jumping at this risky offer as they sought to save their lives before the *Titanic* sank. CEOs often use the *Titanic* trick. In order to sell an unpopular restructuring to their firm, they create a 'burning platform'. They will show that unless drastic action is taken, the firm will go bust or get taken over and everyone will lose their jobs. Suddenly, the unpleasant restructuring looks as attractive as the life rafts of the *Titanic*.

You can use the *Titanic* trick as well. Demonstrate that the cost of doing nothing is greater than the cost of backing you and your idea, and suddenly the risk equation tilts in your favour: colleagues who might be reluctant to support you will join you on the life raft you are offering them.

Summary

- -

By understanding, and using, the trust equation you can build your personal platform for success. Building trust is not a separate activity from your work: it is about how you work. This means it does not take much extra effort, although it will take time: you cannot build trust in a two-minute Zoom call. Becoming the trusted colleague is ➤

at the heart of becoming the colleague of choice. It is your first building block of being able to make impact at scale, beyond your formal power base. Once you know how to become the colleague of choice, you can start to weave your web of influence and informal power, which will greatly amplify your formal power. That is the focus of the next chapter.

-- --

chapter 2

Weave your web: build your network of trusted allies

Discover who you need to build trust with so that you have a powerful network of supporters who can amplify your power. Understand what sort of power you need to succeed and where to find it.

The challenge of harnessing visible and invisible power

If you already know how to build trust, following Chapter 1, you have the core skill required to weave your web of trusted allies and supporters. The next step is to know where to invest your time and effort in building your network.

The obvious place to start is with your line manager, and with the CEO and other key executives who have visible power: money, resources and decision-making rights. You have to master the art of managing your manager. That is a good start, but it is not enough. If that is all you do, you become trapped in the traditional hierarchy where you are competing with many other colleagues for a limited pot of top management time, money and support.

If you want to have real impact, you need the support of colleagues across the organisation. You need to tap into the invisible networks of informal power that make any organisation work in practice. Executives and colleagues with informal power can:

- tell you what is really going on and who is thinking what;
- point you to the right assignments;
- promote and protect your interests when you are not in the room;
- shape how you and your work is perceived;
- help you gain access to key decision makers when you need it.

The more power you have, the more you get. With power you can achieve more, attract more support and grow your network because everyone is attracted to power and success like moths to lamps. That is your opportunity. The problem is how to start: when you have no power or influence, then no one wants to talk to you.

This chapter will show you how to weave an invisible web of influence and support that will let you achieve far more than your formal power and authority would allow. To do this, we will cover three essential topics:

- Find your sponsor.
- Manage your manager.
- Map your power network: find the real sources of power.

Managing your manager is probably the most important skill for you to master. The good news is that if you can manage your manager, you can manage anyone. It is a skill well worth mastering. But we will start elsewhere because there is another role which has the invisible power to transform your career for the better: your sponsor.

If you can manage your manager, you can manage anyone

Find your sponsor

All the big decisions about your career will be taken when you are not in the room. Promotions, bonuses and assignments will be decided at meetings where you are not present. You may not even know that the meeting is happening. This is unnerving, because you should control your destiny. If you don't control your destiny,

All the big decisions about your career will be taken when you are not in the room

someone else will. That 'someone else' may not prioritise your interests, and may not even have your best interests at heart. That raises a fundamental question: *Who is going to be in that room, rooting for you, protecting you and promoting your interests?*

Two conventional answers to this question are not good. The first answer is your manager should be in the room rooting for you. If you are lucky, your manager will be rooting for you. But that is not always the case. At some point you may feel like this beleaguered team member:

> I relied on the integrity and promises of my boss but he let me down. What rankled with me was the public chest thumping and the difference between his words and his actions. These people may have been useless and irresponsible, but they had power. However miserable they are, they can make decisions and never forget that.

There are many reasons they may not support you as much as you would like, because your manager may:

- be weak – faced with other pressures or pushback from colleagues, they choose not to fight the fight for you;
- have other priorities – they may not want to expend valuable social and political capital protecting you and supporting you;
- not want to support you, either because of a style clash or because they want a scapegoat for a problem or because of perceived performance problems;
- favour other team members in preference to you;
- be absent at the vital meeting, for any number of good or less good reasons.

The second conventional answer is you should be able to trust the process. HR systems are designed to be fair, avoid bias and politics and to ensure that you are treated properly. In some firms, the HR system actually works this way. In many more firms, the HR system is not used to make a decision: the HR system is used to justify a decision that has been made on perceptions, emotion and political considerations. The case example below comes from a large professional services firm. It is an extreme example of how informal and invisible rules trump the formal and visible rules.

The HR system is used to justify a decision that has been made on perceptions

The visible and invisible promotion process

The promotions commission sat down to work. There were 30 promotion packs in front of us. Each was a eulogy of praise for outstanding individuals who were being put up for promotion by their managers. The process was tough but transparent. Each promotion pack contained performance appraisals, client testimonials, 360-degree reviews, personal statements and evaluations by multiple managers, all vetted and moderated by HR. So far, so good.

Although there were 30 promotion packs, we had been told that there were only 15 promotions available. This was already a problem: staff had been told that all promotions would be made on merit, regardless of the numbers. We were guaranteed to disappoint 15 very good people who would immediately become flight risks.

The first candidate pack was presented. No one opened the pack: I presumed that was because everyone had read their packs and made their decisions. The chair asked: 'Who knows this candidate?' One partner put her hand up and was effusive in her praise of the candidate, offering detail, evidence and conviction about why promotion was the right decision. The promotion was agreed without further discussion.

The chair asked the same question of the second candidate pack. Another partner muttered: 'Wasn't he the idiot that asked that stupid question at the town hall meeting?' Eyeballs started to roll and others chimed in about personal interactions which they perceived as being no good. After a couple of minutes, that candidate was written off.

No one knew the third candidate, which meant that she was put to the bottom of the pile for further review: if there were any promotion slots left, she would have a chance. We would have to scrutinise her pack in detail, and with some scepticism, given that no one seemed to know her.

➤

> At the end of the meeting, the chair said he would complete the HR formalities. I realised no one had even looked at the promotion criteria the HR team had produced. The chair would simply fill in the HR forms so that they justified the decisions made by the promotions commission.

The lesson from the promotions commission story is that you need someone in the room who is rooting for you when you are not there. That someone is called your 'sponsor', who will normally do far more than be your cheerleader-in-chief when you need it. A good sponsor has two vital characteristics. They are:

1 *Able to help.* They have power and influence to make things happen and to know what is going on;

2 *Willing to help.* They keep your interests at heart, and they have the time and capacity to help you when you need it.

A good sponsor will not only help you at promotion time. They will:

- guide you gently to the right assignments, projects, opportunities and managers;
- protect you when the next round of restructuring comes round;
- let you know how you are really perceived (or ignored) by senior managers;
- alert you to the invisible rules and relationships which can make you or break you;
- have honest conversations with you about how you can do even better.

Children will recognise your sponsor for what he or she really is: your fairy godmother or fairy godfather. When children grow up, they discover that fairy godmothers do not exist. So what chance do you have of finding a fairy godmother in the harsh world of work? And even if they do exist, how can you persuade someone to become your fairy godmother? Someone might become your sponsor because they:

- are nice and want to help;
- need your help;
- are flattered to be asked, and you ask the question.

Are nice and want to help

Most humans are decent, kind and want to help usually. At work, it is easy to forget this. It is hard to see that beyond the grand title and impressive CV, there is a human. This creates problems. If you always treat managers as managers, you create distance and formality. Instead of a personal relationship, you will have a series of professional transactions. You need to look beyond the suit and see the person.

Look beyond the suit and see the person

That senior manager you want as a sponsor was once in your shoes: unsure how to progress and in need of support. They know what it is like for you and are often willing to help, if you ask. For instance, Fiona Dawson is the chair of the Chartered Management Institute and spent 33 years in demanding management roles at Mars. That is a slightly intimidating title and background, but not only is she human, she likes to help:

I adore mentoring younger talent especially younger female talent and in practice I have learned as much from them as they have learned from me. It has been reverse mentoring as much as it has been mentoring.

As ever, giving turns out to be a good way of taking. She mentors, but gains much in return. As we shall see, mentors not only want to help you, but you can help them as well.

Need your help

Senior executives live at the top of the mountain, but have little idea what is happening at the bottom of the mountain. At the top, they see the grand vistas and the future unfolding like the mountain ridges disappearing into the horizon. But they do not know what is happening at the bottom of the mountain that they are responsible for. At the bottom of the mountain you can see what is invisible to them: you see the chickens in the yard, the children in the street and the groceries being delivered. You need senior executives to help you see the big picture; they need you for the detailed picture.

In theory, senior executives can read all the reports that flow up to them to find out what is going on. But reports often do not tell them what they most want to know: what are people thinking, how are customers reacting, what is working well and what is causing problems? They can gain some of this by walking around, which not all executives do. Even then, junior staff rarely have the courage to be honest in public with senior executives: don't give the boss bad medicine.

Adam Smith (not the economist, but an executive who has worked at HSBC and NatWest) recounts the classic story of a typical sponsor, and what the deal was:

> **He would go for coffee with new graduates and junior people and that way he would build his reservoir of stories and knowledge about what was happening and what people were thinking and what they valued. In return he was helping them build their networks. So he had knowledge and perspectives which his peer group did not have. At that level most senior managers just talk to each other. He had something they did not have.**

Senior executives need someone they can trust to fill their knowledge gap reliably. That person could be you. You can give your sponsor a competitive edge over his or her colleagues.

You can give your sponsor a competitive edge over his or her colleagues

Are flattered to be asked, and you ask the question

You probably should not ask a senior executive at your first meeting, 'Will you be my fairy godmother?' You may not get the reaction you want. Instead, identify executives who might be willing and able to help you. If you have a shared background, that often helps: it might be that you have a shared cultural background, or you have a similar education background, or you have shared similar life events and adversity. Not only is it easier to connect with such people, they will understand you better and be more willing to help you. Do your research and you will find a list of potential sponsors.

Your next step is to engineer opportunities to speak with them: water coolers, the edges of meetings and conferences are good moments for you. You can also make yourself useful to them: volunteer to help out on a speech or a project they are preparing. You can then start to grow the relationship organically. In the first instance, ask for some advice about an area where they are expert: they will be flattered to share their expertise with you. Make sure you follow up with a note saying how helpful the advice was, and why it was so helpful. You will quickly discover who is ready to help, and who is not.

The last step is culturally sensitive. In countries with low power distance such as the United States, it is fine to ask a senior executive directly if they will sponsor you. This then gives you explicit permission to continue to ask for advice, and you may well be explicitly asked for information or support in return.

Countries with high power distance, found in much of Asia, have a stronger hierarchy and more respect for authority: everyone knows their place. More power distance makes it harder to make a direct ask. Instead, you have to let the relationship continue to grow organically. At each stage, make sure that your informal sponsor is getting something in return: at minimum gratitude, but perhaps also information and support that they value. A vital part of your role is to make your sponsor look good: they do not want to

> **Your role is to make your sponsor look good**

back a lazy failure who will embarrass them. Sponsorship is a two-way street.

Whatever sort of sponsor you have, use them well. They are busy people and they have many other things to worry about. Ask for their advice and support when you know it will make a real difference, and then make sure they know they have made a difference. Use them well and they will be your fairy godmother, looking out for you at those pivotal moments in your career.

How a sponsor helped the world's worst EA become corporate counsel

Gloria Sanchez successfully moved from a weak starting position to senior counsel at a global professional services firm. She epitomises many of the skills of PQ: she found work where she could shine, she took on the tough stuff, she always delivered. So far, so obvious even if it is hard to achieve. But she realised that this would not be enough to secure her dream role as corporate counsel. She needed a sponsor to help her navigate her way to success. Here is her story:

'I always wanted to become corporate counsel. People told me just do good work. But I knew that was not enough. I knew that if I followed the advice and just did good work that would not help. People would make me do things which I was good at, like organising events. It was tempting to do that because it's easier. If you want to progress your career you have to do difficult and dangerous things from time to time. You cannot always just do the easy things.

I was probably the worst executive assistant they ever had. Expenses would simply not get done.

I had to get business sponsors. Because I was an executive assistant, I plugged into the informal network of executive assistants and made friends with all the executive assistants in the US, although I was based in Mexico. This opened lots of doors. As an executive assistant I got access to senior people

---

and I would ask them endless questions because I knew no answers. I slowly found out which of them would help me and support me.

I found sponsors by making friends. I saw one important person coming from the United States and because I was managing the diary I saw that he had a ten-minute gap in his diary. So I decided to take that time, and I asked him to be my mentor which he agreed to.'

In passing, you might want to note the hidden power of EAs: they are a powerful network of information that has, and guards, access to all the key people in an organisation. Gloria leveraged that to her advantage. By asking questions she was able to find out who was helpful and who was not. From there, it became natural to ask the senior executive to become her sponsor.

Manage your manager, and the CEO

The art of leadership is to make things happen through people you do not control, such as colleagues in other departments and through external stakeholders. The most important stakeholder you do not control is your manager. This makes managing your manager the ideal training ground for

> **The art of leadership is to make things happen through people you do not control**

learning how to make things happen through people you do not control. If you manage your manager well you will:

- enhance and accelerate your career;
- increase your impact, because your manager will trust you, empower you and protect you;
- increase your impact because you will have learned how to make things happen through someone you do not control: your manager.

Managing your manager is about both style and substance. It is also about understanding what your boss really wants from you, which may or may not be related to the formal HR systems of the firm. We will cover each of these three items in this section:

- Understanding what your manager really wants from you.
- Style: how to stay in tune with your manager.
- Substance: always deliver.

Understanding what your manager really wants from you

Performance appraisals cover everything except the most important item: how well you work with your manager. If you work well with your manager, you will find that your performance appraisal is good; a poor working relationship normally leads to a poor appraisal. Understanding what your manager wants, matters.

As a team member, you have to work out what your manager really wants. As a manager, what you want from your team is probably the same as what your manager wants from you. Two broad principles stand out:

- *Make your manager look good.* Deliver great results reliably and focus on what matters to your manager. As one senior executive put it: 'what interests my boss, fascinates me'. Understand what your manager needs to achieve, and help them achieve it.

- *Make life easy for your manager.* Your manager has many things to worry about: do not add yourself to that list if you can avoid it. Don't delegate problems upwards unless there is no other way forward; don't be too needy.

> **Don't delegate problems upwards**

The principles are a good start, but you need more detail. I have asked well over 1,000 managers what they really want from their teams. The answers are consistent. Here are their top five expectations of you and other team members, with the percentage of managers who are satisfied with their team members on each expectation:

1 Hard work (64%)

2 Proactivity (57%)

3 Intelligence (63%)

4 Reliability (61%)

5 Ambition (64%)

These findings are good news: most managers have modest expectations of what good looks like, and more than one in three team members fail to meet those expectations.

To stand out, you do not need to go in search of excellence; you need to go in search of competence. To understand how to succeed with your manager, it is worth understanding what managers mean when they talk about each of their top five expectations.

> **You do not need to go in search of excellence; you need to go in search of competence**

1 *Hard work*. There are few shortcuts to success. Despite what some self-proclaimed gurus preach, you will not succeed by working for four hours a week. The problem is that managers rarely know how much work is hard work. If you are working on a manufacturing line, it is easy to measure productivity and quality. Working in the office above the manufacturing line, it is more or less impossible to measure productivity and quality: work is too ambiguous, open ended, complex and variable. The problem is even worse with hybrid work. In the office, your manager can see if you appear to be working hard and if you look like you are suffering from too much pressure or stress. When you are remote, your manager does not know if you are working all hours, or if you are spending all day practising the banjo. In practice, this means you have to sell your work to your manager. You have to make it clear

> **Sell your work to your manager**

what you are doing, how long it is taking, what obstacles you face and what help you need. A simple discipline is to hold a daily briefing with him or her, ideally at the start of the day. This meeting is called a YTB meeting when done by hybrid teams working on IT development sprints. YTB stands for:

- Y: *yesterday. This is what I did yesterday.* This confirms that you did what you agreed to do.

- T: *today. This is what I will do today.* This ensures you are seen to be working on the right thing and doing the right amount of work. This is where you can sell your effort and commitment to your manager by making sure he or she understands the entirety of your agenda.

- B: *blockers. These are the blockers which might derail my work.* This leads to a constructive conversation about where your manager might help. It also alerts your manager to potential risks.

These YTB briefings need only take two minutes per team member. It is quick for everyone on the team to get up to speed. If there are significant problems to be resolved, that can lead to a longer conversation later.

2 *Proactivity.* Managers like delegation to be a one-way street. They want to delegate work to you, and they want you to take care of it. They do not want you delegating problems back up to them. They want you to take the initiative and sort out problems yourself, because they do not have the time to deal with your problems as well as theirs and everyone else's. That is the minimum proactivity they want. But they usually want more. The best team members go further and suggest ideas, seize opportunities and spot risks and problems early on. Managers want you to be proactive, to lead and to make more impact: they want you to step up while followers step back into the safety of following the herd.

3 *Intelligence.* In the past managers were meant to solve all the toughest problems of the team: they were meant to be the

smartest person in the room. Forty years ago, this might have been true because only one in ten adults held degrees. The world has changed. As a manager you do not have to be the smartest person in the room: your job is to get the smartest people into the room. Fortunately, managers do not expect you to be Einstein on steroids.

> **You do not have to be the smartest person in the room: your job is to get the smartest people into the room**

They just need you to apply your common sense, expertise and experience to find solutions to all the messy and complicated problems that work entails. Once again, good managers are giving you licence to take control, use your intelligence and make an impact.

4 *Reliability.* Managers hate surprises because they are rarely good. If your manager is caught by surprise, you make them look bad in front of their peers: it looks like they are not in control and they are not managing properly.

> **Managers hate surprises because they are rarely good**

Reliability is not just about delivering the right outcomes at the right time. It is also about delivering the right information at the right time. This can be very tricky in cultures where you are not meant to give the boss bad medicine. This means bad news is suppressed until everything blows up. If you hold daily YTB meetings (see above) with your manager, then you can raise problems and blockers early in a constructive way by asking for help and support under the Blockers agenda item.

5 *Ambition* was the surprise finding. As we saw in Chapter 1, there are two flavours of ambition: personal ambition and ambition for the mission. Personal ambition is fine: you show hunger and drive, and you will be more proactive and productive as a result. But it can also make you a high-maintenance team member, which most managers could live without. What they really want is ambition for the mission and for the team: they want team members who go above and beyond, take on discretionary work and do the non-promotable work that keeps teams ticking.

If you display these five characteristics, your manager will support you; your performance appraisal will be good, whatever the formal HR criteria may be; you will be first in line for promotion. In Chapter 7 you will discover that promotions are not entirely rational. The formal HR processes are not used to make a rational decision. The HR process is used to justify a decision which has been made on political and emotional grounds.

The unwritten rules of managing your boss

Here is a classic response to the question, 'What do you really look for in your team?' The answer came from David Stephen, who has served as chief risk officer at both NatWest and Westpac.

'What I look for in middle leaders is having drive and giving it an honest go. I want to see that they make the effort. I know they cannot be right all the time and so I want to make it safe for them to take a risk and to fail occasionally. Obviously if they fail all the time that is a different matter. I judged the effort not just the outcome. But different leaders will have different criteria for how they judge middle managers.

What else am I looking for in middle managers?

- Show that you are motivated by team success, not just by self-success.

- Have you solved the problem? Or are you dealing with minor matters?

- You must groom your replacements. You must have three people who would be able to step into your shoes because senior people must be able to develop other people.

- Do you share the credit or take the credit, and do you take the blame or point the blame?

> Naturally none of us will challenge the formal HR evaluation criteria. That is not a battle worth fighting. Instead we all talk about the extra criteria or the special criteria that we are looking for in our area.'
> How do you perform against the unwritten rules of success?

As well as asking managers what they most wanted from their team members, I also asked what they did not want. Knowing how to avoid messing up is as important as knowing how to succeed. The good news is that most managers are reasonably forgiving. If you have bad taste and bad jokes and the occasional bad day, they will forgive that. There are good reasons why most managers are forgiving:

Most managers are reasonably forgiving

- They have been in your shoes before and know what it is like to be human (surprisingly).

- Most managers are conflict averse: they only fight battles if they have to.

- They need to keep a good team well-motivated.

But there is one thing that few managers ever forgive: disloyalty. Disloyalty is not just about plotting to stab your manager in the back and take their position. Disloyalty is as simple as failing to stand up for your manager in a meeting where things are going awry; it is about failing to disclose information resulting in a nasty surprise for your boss. It is also, as one slightly defensive manager put it: 'Don't outshine me, don't outsmart me and don't outflank me.'

These invisible and political rules of survival and success are universal. Even the Church can be intensely political. Here is Matteo talking about the arrival of a new manager at his business in Italy. As a priest, his business is the Church and his manager is called a bishop.

'The new Bishop was threatened by me because I could do more and achieve more than he did. So I was outshining him. He felt he was being upstaged.' Matteo's error was to build his parish congregation and have a sellout attendance at Easter Mass. Unwisely, he celebrated his success in an interview with a local radio station. The reporter compared Matteo's success with the falling attendance at the bishop's cathedral. That turned out to be a career limiting move for Matteo, who found that his manager was now his enemy.

A confident manager would probably celebrate the success of a team member. A more traditional command and control manager will resent being outshone by a subordinate and regard that as deeply disloyal.

Disloyalty breaks the bond of trust that you need between yourself and your manager. Once the trust is gone, the relationship is gone. It may take a few days or weeks or even months, but there will be a parting of ways. Your manager is unlikely to engineer a good exit for you. Matteo soon found himself parting ways with his bishop and starting again with a new community.

Style: how to stay in tune with your manager

Many conflicts within teams are about style, not substance. In theory, there is no right or wrong style. Popular psychological tests such as MB/TI® (Myers-Briggs Type Indicators®) are a simple way of showing how everyone has a different way of working, and they can all be effective in different contexts. But in practice, if you and your manager have very different ways of working you will discover that there is one right way: your manager's way. Your manager is unlikely to adjust a long-established way of working for the different style of each team member. If you want to avoid unnecessary conflict, it pays to work with the style of your manager. Doing this can be the difference between success and failure, as you will see in Lenny's case study below.

> **Many conflicts within teams are about style, not substance**

Managing the unmanageable manager

Lenny was an entrepreneurial and mercurial CEO. Each Monday morning, he would rush into the office, having been wound up by all the ideas he had over the weekend. He was a coruscating whirl of activity: setting direction, asking questions, demanding answers and making things happen at speed. No one knew how to manage him beyond keeping out of his way and doing as he said. It was impossible to get a word in edgeways with him, especially at the start of the week.

Over the week, he would slowly wind down. By Friday afternoon everyone would be exhausted by the week and by him: most staff left early. Lenny would finally relax. It was the ideal time to wander into his office and have a relaxed chat about whatever was top of mind. For the first time in the week he would be in listening mode, not broadcast mode. Planting ideas in his head on a Friday gave them time to mature over the weekend so that they became reality on Monday morning.

Every boss is unique. It would be easy to mock Lenny's style, and many staff did just that over a beer on Friday evening. Judging people is easy, understanding them is harder but more useful. The judgement on Lenny was that he was manic and impossible to manage. Understanding him meant staying until late on Friday creating the chance to have a productive and reflective conversation that could shape his agenda.

In the case of Lenny, the key insight was that it was pointless having a thoughtful conversation with him on Monday mornings, but Friday evenings were the ideal time to plant ideas with him. There is no psychometric test that will ever reveal a stylistic detail like that. You have to observe your manager's style closely, observe how colleagues and peers deal with him or her, and try different strategies yourself.

Aside from the Monday versus Friday style difference, here are some typical style differences you may want to look out for:

- morning versus afternoon;
- big picture versus detail;
- tasks versus people focus;
- empowering versus controlling;
- numbers versus ideas;
- deductive versus inductive thinking;
- risk taking versus risk averse;
- outcome focus versus process focus.

If you like to work the detail and the numbers, focus on the tasks and avoid unnecessary risk, you will need to adjust your style dramatically if your boss likes to focus on the big idea, deal with the people and take risks to achieve big outcomes. Neither of you are right or wrong, but it is up to you to find a way to communicate with your manager so that you are understood.

Learning to work with different styles is relevant not only to working with your manager. It is relevant to working with all those other people you need to influence: colleagues, peers and external stakeholders. If you have style clashes with them all, you will find it hard to build the alliances you need to make an impact.

To succeed through people you do not control, including your manager, you need to adjust to their style of working. This is always a tricky balancing act. You are who you are: you should play to your strengths and be true to yourself. Stay authentic. But if you know that the person you are dealing with is a deductive thinker (starts with the big idea and then works to the detail) then you will not succeed with inductive thinking (working from the detail to the grand conclusion). Communicate in a way that they will understand.

Substance: always deliver

How do you know if any of your colleagues are succeeding? How will they know if you are succeeding? Very often, style becomes substance. If you see a colleague who appears to be full of confidence and highly motivated, it is easy to assume that they must be doing very well. Equally, a colleague who appears to be depressed and lacking in any confidence will probably be seen to be struggling. Perceptions can be dangerous: never confuse confidence with competence. Perceptions may be false, but the consequences of perceptions are always real. Manage perceptions well: if you project confidence and seem motivated, others will assume you are doing well.

> **Never confuse confidence with competence.**

> **Perceptions may be false, but the consequences of perceptions are always real**

We should not judge books by their covers, nor people by their appearances. But we do. Turn this to your advantage.

It may seem very shallow to judge people by how they behave, but that is a natural consequence of work today. Four things make it very hard to judge how well anyone is performing:

- Ambiguous, variable and complex work makes it very hard to judge how much effort a piece of work requires, and how well it was done.

- Shared, diffused responsibility makes it easy to hide but hard to shine. Failure may feel a very lonely place, but success is usually a very crowded place. Spotting who was really responsible for what can be hard.

- Hybrid work makes it harder for colleagues and managers to see what you are doing and how you are performing. It also makes it harder for you to have those short, informal chats and accidental encounters which help you sell your story, get advice and build alliances.

- Not-for-profit organisations, including the public sector, struggle even more with performance. Profit is a useful mediator of decision making and appraisals in the for-profit sector: there is no equivalent mediator in the not-for-profit sector.

Despite all this, performance matters. If you have a gold medal in idleness or incompetence, you will be noticed: no amount of confidence or bluster will save you. At the other extreme, gold medallist high performers get noticed because they normally have some exceptional claim to fame. Once you become known for something, you grow your credibility, accelerate your career and extend your network. How you can achieve your claim to fame is covered in Chapter 3.

In practice, few people are gold medallists, either for incompetence or achievement. We have to live in the grey space of performance. You know how hard you have worked and you know what you have achieved, but colleagues and managers will not know what you know. This means you have to sell your achievements and sell your effort, without being the office jerk who is always bragging and annoying everyone else.

You can use two tried-and-tested methods to ensure your performance is recognised properly. Both methods have already been covered:

- *Daily YTB briefings with your manager and your colleagues.* When your manager is aware of what you did yesterday (Y), what you are doing today (T) and the blockers you have overcome (B) he or she will be acutely aware of your performance. You may find it sensible to add a monthly check-in with your manager. Ostensibly, this can be about work priorities and focus. In practice, it is a good way to make sure your manager knows what you are achieving and what sort of work you want to stay focused on. Regular check-ins will keep your manager happy and ensure that your formal appraisal contains no surprises.

- *Spread the glory.* When you have a success, be very generous in your praise to everyone who helped. Make sure your manager knows about all these helpful colleagues. More importantly, make sure the managers of all your colleagues know how brilliant they have been. Trumpet the success of everyone else loudly and widely. By giving away the praise, you demonstrate that you were the person who was at the centre of the success. You gain praise by giving it away. A variation of this is to do a formal review of the success to extract the lessons learned. This is useful in its own right, and it amplifies your success.

YTB briefings and spreading the glory are good ways to highlight your performance, especially when you are in the grey space of performance. But the best way to demonstrate that you can deliver is to break out of the grey space and build a distinctive claim to fame which is recognised across the organisation and at least two levels up the hierarchy.

Map your power network

Your power network is how you amplify your formal power through an informal network of trusted allies and supporters. Senior executives have this: they know who to call and how to work with other senior executives they have known for years. Often, they fail to realise the importance of this network until they jump ship and join another firm. Suddenly, they discover that they have no informal power network to call upon, and making anything happen is very difficult. Network analysis by Rob Cross shows that it typically takes senior executives three to five years to replicate their power networks in a new organisation. Many fail to achieve this and leave because they can no longer make an impact without their power network. Building your own power network is vital to your success.

> **Building your own power network is vital to your success**

53

You need the right people in your network: quality, not size, matters: 10,000 followers on LinkedIn will not help you if your colleagues in finance, HR, IT and legal do not support you.

A simple way to map your required network is a variation of the RACI tool used on most projects. This identifies who is responsible, accountable, consulted and informed on your project. There are endless variations of this tool, but they help clarify who needs to be involved and how. At risk of acronym overload, the variation of RACI, which you need for your power network, is GRACIE. Gracie is your friend and stands for:

1 *Gatekeepers:* they open, or close, doors for you and help you gain the access you need;

2 *Responsible:* this is you, because only you can be responsible for you;

3 *Authorisers* come in two flavours: your direct manager(s) and staff in other departments who can approve or block your ideas;

4 *Collaborators:* this includes your team, but also colleagues, clients and suppliers who you work with to make things happen;

5 *Influencers* may hold little formal power but they can sway opinion for or against you;

6 *Executive sponsor:* your sponsor is an influencer on steroids and is rooting for you. Other influencers may or may not support you.

If we were listing these people in terms of importance, we would start with you (R) and then the authorisers (A) and then argue about the others until finishing with the influencers. That would lead to a very ugly acronym such as RACEGI which is impossible to remember. Using literary licence, we will stick with our trusty friend GRACIE and explore each role in a little more detail.

Use GRACIE to map your power network: how widely are you connected and how strong is each connection? A strong connection is one where:

- you know the person well; you understand their personal and professional background, and how they like to work;

- they are responsive and always answer your messages positively;

- they reach out to you proactively and keep you informed. They act as your early warning radar system;
- they support you: they will expedite your requests, prioritise your work and open doors for you.

Inevitably, you will find gaps in your power network. That is the point of mapping it, so you can make the connections you need to. Invest in these relationships early. If you rush to these power sources at the last moment demanding help and support, you will find that you lack the social or political capital to make things happen.

As you build your power map, you will discover that some executives can hold multiple GRACIE roles.

Here is each role in more detail.

1 *Gatekeepers* can help or hinder you. You can find three types of gatekeeper:

- executive assistants;
- super connectors;
- ransom seekers.

Executive assistants are the classic gatekeepers. A trusted EA will control the diary of an executive and prioritise what the executive sees. They know the executive's priorities and act accordingly. If you treat the EA with respect and as a professional, you are far more likely to succeed than if you treat the EA as a low-level servant. And EAs tend to form a strong network which can span the globe: if you annoy one EA, you annoy the entire network. Your reputation precedes you: treat all EAs with the professional courtesy and respect they deserve.

Your reputation precedes you

Super connectors bridge functions, business units and the hierarchy. Sometimes this is because of their role. People in HR, finance and planning see across the whole organisation. But other connectors have a wide network because they are respected for their knowledge, wisdom and expertise. Super connectors tend to be supportive, which is partly why they are so well connected. Find them, build your relationship with them early: do not demand that they open doors for you on your first meeting with them.

Ransom seekers claim to be gatekeepers: in practice they close gates rather than open them. These are often mid-level executives who claim to be able to open the vital door for you. But in return they just want you to change this bit of your plan, and that bit, and another bit, and help out on this and that. They hold you to ransom until you discover that they are either unable or unwilling to open the door you want. Never rely on just one door opener, because then you become dependent. With multiple door openers, you can bypass anyone who tries to hold you to ransom.

The power of EAs

The firm had a rigorous recruitment process which included psychometric tests, extensive interviews, cases and a sample presentation. But there was only one test which reliably indicated whether someone was worth recruiting or not: my EA.

Nikki would greet candidates on arrival and shepherd them into their interviews. It took four or five minutes to take the elevator and reach the interview suite. In that time, candidates routinely revealed themselves, because they thought they were not being observed. Some candidates were nervous, which was fair enough. Some ignored Nikki or condescended to her; some were smart enough to ask her questions about the firm and the process; some treated her with respect and others did not.

After the formal reviews were complete, I would ask Nikki for her verdict. Nearly always, her verdict and the official verdict were the same. On the few occasions when there was a difference, Nikki's verdict normally proved to be the most accurate.

Never underestimate the power or influence of a good EA.

2 *Responsible.* You are the responsible executive. You are responsible for your career, how you are perceived, how you perform, how you behave, how you feel. This is not a burden: this is liberating. It is about taking control of your destiny, taking control of how you feel and act. If you let the system determine your destiny and let events determine your feelings, you become a victim of fate which can be kind, or very cruel.

3 *Authorisers* are powerful and probably have little time for your project. Manage them well. Your most important authoriser is your manager. We have already covered how you can manage your manager, and what your manager expects from you. Other authorisers have negative power: they cannot approve your plans, but they can veto your plans. Staff in finance, HR, legal, risk, health and safety have important roles to do: they stop the firm getting into trouble. You are likely to change your view of them over time. Early in your career you may be frustrated by their ability to say no, to delay you and demand changes to your plans. Later in your career you rely on these same people to stop bad stuff happening by mistake. Involve them early in your thinking so that you can shape your plans in a way which works from their perspective. Work with them, not against them.

4 *Collaborators* are the people whose help you need to make things happen. For traditional managers, this meant their team. But in today's world, you need the active support of people you do not control in marketing, operations, sales, IT and elsewhere. Build these relationships early. If you go to them with a last-minute demand for help, do not be surprised if you find yourself at the back of the queue. These functions often have demands which exceed their capacity, and everyone is claiming that their need is the most important and urgent. For instance, in advertising agencies the account managers deal with the clients and translate the clients' needs into a creative brief. The creative side is usually overwhelmed with demands. If you have a good relationship, you will get good creatives who give you proper time. If you have no relationship or a poor relationship, your demands will not be

a priority: if you get support, it may well be from junior and/or untried creatives.

5 *Influencers* are the most mysterious power source. They have no formal role in decision making, but they can shape how you and your proposal is seen. Your customers are the classic and most powerful influencer. Bring the voice of the customer in support of your plan, and you will find you have a powerful ally. Consultants also wield great influence. Whether you like them or dislike them, set aside your personal feelings and use their influence to support you. Work with them and help them: make them your allies, not your enemies. Within your firm, super connectors are not only door openers, they are influencers because people respect them and listen to them. Tap into the invisible networks of power and influence.

6 *Executive sponsors* have been covered at length already. They are your fairy godmother or godfather who will be rooting for you when it matters. One fairy godmother is good, two is better: you need cover in case one fairy godmother falls ill, is away on business, moves to a different business unit or firm or is just plain unavailable at the moment the key meeting happens.

In the soup

A short trip into the esoteric world of soup tin labels will show the importance of tapping into the power of influencers. Frances worked for a large paper company: one of the many product lines she had responsibility for was soup labels which she sold to a major soup manufacturer. The relationship was typical and it was not good. The buyer always wanted lower prices, and Frances was always under pressure to deliver higher prices. The result would normally be a verbal wrestling match: buyer power versus supplier power. Formal power fights formal power.

One day, Frances made a surprising request: could she meet some of the people who actually used her soup labels? The buyer agreed. And over the next few weeks she discovered that there is more to soup labels than just price:

- The buying department was measured on price reductions, hence the constant verbal wrestling on price. The way to deliver low prices was to do very long runs of the same sort of label on a fixed schedule. That maximised efficiency, but was not what the rest of the soup firm wanted.

- Manufacturing and distribution really did not care about price, because the soup label was a negligible part of their costs. What they cared about was availability: if they ran out of soup labels, their entire operation would come to a halt, just because of a minor component. They did not want to have large amounts of soup label inventory in the factory: they wanted the labels available on demand.

- Marketing did not care about price either. They wanted short runs of soup for test markets, for promotions and for the very high margin special editions and special flavours. Long fixed runs of tomato soup labels were stopping Marketing from marketing.

- Sales also did not care about price. What they wanted was flexibility and speed. If a marketing promotion succeeded, they needed to get extra volumes into the trade very quickly otherwise there would be empty shelves and they would lose sales.

Frances had tapped into a network of invisible influencers: they welcomed Frances because they had not been able to wield any influence over buying before. They were all stuck with long fixed runs which were not helping them. She had also found a way of making the buyer look great without focusing 100 per cent on price.

The solution they came up with was elegant. Frances's paper company had some new factories which could produce long

> runs at very low cost, meeting the tomato soup challenge. But those factories were designed for long runs; short runs wrecked their efficiency with changeover times. The paper company also had some older factories which were slightly less efficient, but far more flexible: they could produce the short runs at short notice for higher prices. Everyone was happy, for a while.

Summary

Becoming the colleague of choice and weaving your web of influence and power are the essential foundations of having impact. They are investments which will pay dividends repeatedly for you by allowing you to escape the confines of the hierarchy and make impact far beyond the limits of your formal power and authority. The next challenge is to make sure that you are working on the right agenda, which is the focus of the next chapter.

chapter 3

Work smart, not just hard: work on the right agenda

This chapter shows how the right agenda will enable you to have great impact, regardless of your seniority. You will gain exposure, build credibility and accelerate your career. The challenge is to find the right agenda, build it and balance it with your day job.

The challenge of the right agenda

How will you be remembered? Being remembered for how you are is both easy and inevitable. Being remembered for what you do is vital but hard.

How will you be remembered?

For a moment, think back on some of the managers or teachers you have had. The chances are that you remember little of what they achieved. You will certainly not recall whether they beat budget by 6.7 per cent three years ago, even if that was an epic achievement against the odds for them. Although their achievements will be as clear as a muddy pond, you will recall what they were like with crystal clarity.

If you are going to be remembered more for how you are than for what you do, choose well. If you want to be remembered as the positive, proactive, ambitious, intelligent and reliable team member that managers look for, what evidence can you provide to prove that? What else can you do over the next day, week, month or year?

But even if you look and act the part, at some point you have to deliver the goods. The most successful managers don't just look good, you have to have impact which goes far beyond your span of control.

The last two chapters prepared the ground. They showed how you can become the colleague of choice, and how you can build a web of influence and trusted allies around the organisation. This gives you informal power which can greatly amplify your formal power. But the golden rule of power is this: use it or lose it.

If you are only a colleague of choice with a network of allies, then you are nice but harmless. You become a super connector of colleagues, a confidante of peers and managers and you will be widely liked. You will be remembered well after you are eased out in a restructuring. However much you are liked, you will not survive unless you have impact. You have to pass the key leadership test: can you take people where they would not have got by themselves?

Can you take people where they would not have got by themselves?

Being remembered for what you do instead of how you are is hard. Look around your colleagues and managers: you know what they are like, but you may find it hard to identify a distinctive achievement that any of them have had. The few that have a distinctive achievement are themselves distinctive. They are one of the few that are likely to go far. So how can you become one of the few with distinctive impact, rather than one of the many striving to beat this quarter's budget?

Having a distinctive claim to fame is essential for your long-term career. It gives you a platform, visibility and credibility. It makes you stand out from your peers and it shows you can have real impact.

Working on business-as-usual is already hard work. The demands of work never get less: the organisation always demands more output for less resource. As a result, you can feel like a hamster spinning on an accelerating wheel to nowhere. The harder you run, the faster the wheel spins and you still land up in the same place that you started.

Many managers mistake activity for achievement. You can occasionally see them, running between meetings while taking a call and checking their notes and giving some quality time to

Many managers mistake activity for achievement

a colleague they meet in the corridor while juggling a cup of coffee. They are a coruscating whirl of activity. But at year end, what have they achieved?

Never mistake activity for achievement

Charles Darwin was a Victorian gentleman of leisure. He secured a self-funded place on HMS *Beagle* as the resident naturalist. He spent the next five years, from 1831 to 1836, essentially pottering around the world making observations of all the things that might gain the attention of a gentleman naturalist. Among other things, he noticed the different sorts of finches' beaks on different islands in the Galapagos: an interesting, but potentially irrelevant, curiosity.

After he returned to England, he appeared to do nothing very much for 20 years. He did not multitask between email, video conferencing, preparing PowerPoint presentations while working on a spreadsheet all at the same time, partly because none of these things had been invented. But he continued to think about those finches' beaks and the other curiosities he had observed.

Eventually, his friends persuaded him to publish his thoughts. His book, *On the Origin of Species*, was published in 1859. It was a bombshell which changed everything: how we thought about ourselves as humans and about how species adapt, evolve and perish. It was also an onslaught on traditional religious orthodoxy of the time.

Achievement is not about activity or hyperactivity: it is about working on the right agenda and seeing it through to completion.

All of the successful managers who took part in the original research for this book worked hard. But they were not just spinning the hamster wheel faster and faster. They were moving ahead: the wheel was taking them where they wanted to go, rather than staying in place. The key to their success was that they worked on the right agenda.

Finding the right agenda is the key to success because it helps you:

- achieve impact;
- be remembered for what you do, not just how you are;
- accelerate your career by having a claim to fame;
- build credibility by showing what you can do;
- enhance your informal power by becoming noticed and a go-to person for challenges and opportunities;
- become visible to senior management;
- set yourself apart from your activity-focused peers;

- take control by working on your agenda, not an agenda that is given to you;
- learn at speed about how to make things happen, have impact and make change.

Having an agenda which has meaning and purpose for you is also a great way to sustain your motivation and productivity. If you own your work, you blast through all the routine and noise of daily work so that you can create the time to focus on what matters most to you: your big idea. It is better to make your agenda than to take the agenda from someone else.

Finding your impact agenda

The best book you never need to read is called *Take Control of Your Destiny, or Someone Else Will*. The reason you do not need to read it is that the message is in the title. If someone else controls your destiny and controls your agenda, at best you can hope to get lucky with your assignments. But hope is not a method and luck is not a strategy. If you let the organisation decide your destiny, you will probably be required to work on some form of business-as-usual. You will be required to get onto the hamster wheel and start spinning it as fast as you can. You may or may not be able to spin faster than your colleagues, but you will find it very hard to stand out from everyone else who is also spinning their wheel.

Hope is not a method and luck is not a strategy

The most outstanding managers who took part in the original research for this book all took control of their destiny. They all found a distinctive agenda which they could call their own and where they could make a distinctive impact. There was a pattern to how they did this, and it is a pattern you can copy if you want to. To make an impact you can choose to:

1 tackle assignments that no one else wants to work on;
2 create a new agenda which no one has worked on;

3 challenge orthodoxy of an existing agenda;

4 step up in a crisis;

5 work on the CEO's agenda.

If you think of your career in strategic terms, your choices have strong echoes of both strategic intent (CK Prahalad and Gary Hamel) and blue ocean strategy (Chan Kim and Renée Mauborgne). Both theories advocate that firms are most likely to win where there is no competition or little competition. In your career you are most likely to succeed where you face little or no competition from colleagues.

This section will show how you can build your distinctive impact agenda around your choice from the five above.

1. Tackle assignments that no one else wants to work on

The CEO made me an offer: would I like a one-way ticket to Japan? The opportunity I had to solve was the Japanese business which had no sales, no income and no clients but plenty of bills to pay. And I had no Japanese language skills. Curiously, no one else seemed very keen on this opportunity. It was the chance to run a proper business for the first time, a big step up. So I took up the offer and my life changed. Along the way, I made several important discoveries:

- Tough assignments are tough: hard work, pressure and stress.

- No one else wants to work on them for good reason. They accelerate your career: you succeed fast or you fail fast.

- You learn a huge amount. You live life in technicolor, and with the record button on.

- You can have great impact and build a lasting claim to fame.

High-impact managers do not wait for the tough stuff to come to them, they actively seek it out. These are roles where you can make a distinctive impact fast. For instance, Maddy Storr took on the role of selling a software product for a global firm into Switzerland and Germany. It was a combination of product and geography that no one else wanted. She achieved 720 per cent of her quota and became salesperson of the year. It was an easy quota to beat: because there had been minimal sales before, she was starting from a very low base. That kickstarted her career and she has progressed from account manager to SVP in eight years, making the vital transition from salesperson to manager and leader along the way.

Wherever you are, there are challenges no one wants to address. This is your blue ocean: you can make an impact by going where no one else dares to go. For instance, Google was facing a challenge on apprenticeships. Switzerland issued large fines to firms that did not deliver apprenticeships; the UK introduced an apprenticeship levy on payrolls which strongly encouraged firms like Google to invest in apprenticeships. Google is mainly in the search business; it is not in the apprenticeship business. And if you are in California seeing all these disparate rules and regulations coming into force around apprenticeships, you probably just want the problem to go away: you have more pressing matters to deal with.

Around this time, Amanda Timberg joined Google to lead their entry-level recruiting across EMEA, following her successful experience in building Teach First in the UK. She also saw three things:

- Many governments were keen to push apprenticeships for young people who do not go to university.

- Google was in a strong position to champion apprenticeships as strong pathways to meaningful careers.

- No one at Google wanted to touch apprenticeships. They were complicated and messy and the business case to invest was not immediately clear.

So Amanda just took control. She set up an internal website for apprenticeships, set out three rules for all global apprenticeship programmes and started answering questions to help people around the world. Each question generated an answer which appeared on the website, and she quickly became the global authority on apprenticeships.

Amanda did all of this under the radar: her initial budget was small and could be hidden. She had no global authority, but became one simply by taking the lead. Google now has successful apprentice-ship programmes around the world.

If you work on business-as-usual, it is hard to shine. Everyone else is also working hard to make their numbers. If you take on the tough stuff, you have a chance to make a real impact across the entire organisation, even if you are new to the firm and the organisation is one of the largest on the planet: Google.

> **If you work on business-as-usual, it is hard to shine**

The United Nations may not save the world, but may save your job

Dreamforce is Salesforce's annual flagship event which draws in 140,000 people. Making it successful is a huge effort for Salesforce management. It usually conflicts with another big global event: UNGA, the United Nations General Assembly. As a global player, Salesforce needed to be present and effective at UNGA. It was an orphan in search of a caring parent. This was the moment for Nancy De Vore to step up. In her words:

'The UN General Assembly was a hot potato and no one was touching it. No one else wanted to go near it because they all wanted to focus on Dreamforce and get exposure to Marc Benioff (Salesforce founder) and all the other important people who would go there.

I started working on the UN General Assembly on the side. It was not my day job. I had no budget for the UN General Assembly. But I was getting myself invited to things. So I got a call together to find out who was doing what at the UN General Assembly. I found out that there was good stuff going on, so I said how do we make this even better next year? And they replied, "Why don't you make it happen?" I was a bit naïve and I just took it on and then I became the leader.

If it had gone across to Marketing then they would start marketing, and the UN General Assembly would tell us to get

> lost because they do not want selling. My job is not to sell. It is to amplify the work of the UN and in time they will acknowledge us and we will become a trusted partner to them.
>
> No one else focuses on the UN General Assembly. I quickly came to own this. If you asked Mark Benioff he would say, "Oh yes Nancy owns that. And if she steps out then there is no one else who would pick it up."
>
> In a recent restructuring, the entire team was eliminated except for me. All of my colleagues who were fired were exceptional and had very good skills, but it was the UN General Assembly that saved me.'
>
> Working on matters which no one else wants to touch makes you indispensable, as well as enabling you to make a distinctive impact and have a distinctive claim to fame.

2. Create a new agenda which no one has worked on

If taking on a tough agenda that no one else wants is unattractive, you can instead create your own agenda. This is like being an entrepreneur within your organisation. Being entre-

Create your own agenda

preneurial within an organisation carries significant advantages because you:

- have an established network that you can plug into;
- do not need to worry about making month end pay roll;
- can rely on a machine to manage all the IT, finance, HR and legal that you take for granted within a firm but becomes very burdensome when you are outside the firm.

The downside is that it can be a struggle to gain acceptance for your idea, especially in the larger machine bureaucracies which value stability and efficiency more than innovation and risk. Chapter 4 will show, with practical examples, how you can sell your idea within the firm. It is easier to go from idea to impact when you have the support of an existing firm instead of having to build a new firm.

3. Challenge orthodoxy of an existing agenda

Leadership is about taking people where they would not have got by themselves. If you always follow orthodoxy, you never challenge the existing way of doing things and stick to the existing agenda you can still be a good manager, but you will not be a leader. You need leaders to lead the revolution, but you need managers to make sure that the trains run on time and the bread gets delivered before, during and after the revolution. People remember the leaders, not the managers, of revolutions. To make an impact, be ready to step up to the challenge of change. You need courage and conviction to challenge the way things are, and to take risks.

Performance management systems make it hard to take risks and innovate, until you are in a crisis. The tyranny of MBO (management by objectives) means that survival is about hitting your targets, which makes most managers risk averse. Risk aversion increases with seniority. Making your numbers this quarter depends on having a smooth-running machine: you cannot have a smooth-running machine if you choose to dismantle it and rebuild it half-way through the quarter. The new machine may be much better, but you may miss this quarter's numbers or even this year's numbers. The bigger the machine you run, the riskier it becomes to change it: it is just too big and complex for a quick fix.

In practice, there are three circumstances which make it easier to challenge orthodoxy. These are when you are:

- *CEO*, because the CEO makes the rules and decides what success looks like. The board will want to see that the CEO is making a difference: otherwise, what is the point of the CEO? Innovation and challenge are part of the CEO's role.

- *Part of a team or firm in a crisis.* A crisis shows that business-as-usual is not working and cannot work. You have to challenge orthodoxy. Crises are a wonderful opportunity for good managers to make an impact.

- *Relatively junior,* when the risk–return trade-off for challenging orthodoxy tilts in your favour.

Being junior should never stop you making an impact. Seniority makes it easier to have impact, but you can have impact at any level if you have a good idea. For instance, Doug Strycharczyk started out as a junior staff member

> **Being junior should never stop you making an impact**

at fine china maker Wedgwood. As part of his development, he was sent to work with a manager at Wedgwood's Coalport business. Most managers stayed in their offices pushing papers. But Doug learned from his manager the value of walking around the shop floor and talking to everyone who was making the china. It was a good way to learn the business. He was new to the ceramics world, so he asked lots of questions and found out just how hierarchical the business was. Challenging tradition was not encouraged. For instance, the stillages (storage racks for pottery) had not changed in design in 150 years. It was assumed that if it had worked for 150 years, it would work for another 150 years. But no one had asked if it could work better, until Doug came along.

Doug saw that all the shelves on the stillage were 18 inches apart, but 95 per cent of the products were less than 4.5 inches high. There was huge waste of space, which led to increased distances to move products around, which cost time and money. He also saw that the bottom shelf was awkward to use and was likely to cause back problems. He made a simple suggestion: reduce the distance between shelves and eliminate the bottom shelf. At a stroke, he changed 150 years of operating history. The change worked, and within a year had spread to most of Wedgwood's 21 other potteries. Doug had an impact and made his name, even as a junior newcomer.

However well established and successful a business may be, there is always opportunity to do things better. If you are junior, that probably means you are working on the front line. Because you are at the bottom of the mountain, you see things which managers at the top of the mountain cannot see. You can see what is not working and what can work even better. You can make an impact by having the courage to speak up and suggest a better way.

> **Make an impact by having the courage to speak up and suggest a better way**

Impact without power: the mysterious case of the missing wheelchairs

Hospitals need wheelchairs in the right place at the right time. This very low-tech piece of kit is vital to making sure all the high-tech kit and highly qualified staff can do their jobs properly. If the wheelchairs are in the wrong place at the wrong time, patients don't get moved to and from operating theatres and wards promptly, causing delays, backlogs and chaos.

Alastair Higginbottom started his career as a hospital porter and experienced the wheelchair challenge first-hand. Patients, surgeons, nurses and staff would all get very upset because the wheelchairs were not in the right place and they could not move patients at the right time.

Alastair and the other porters felt the problem acutely as they would feel the wrath of the surgeons when things went wrong.

'I decided to fix the problem without permission. All the porters were going crazy because there were no wheelchairs ever available at one end of the hospital. That was management policy. So over one week I decided to start hiding a cache of wheelchairs at that end of the hospital. I did that without permission. By the end of the week, we had a bank of wheelchairs which porters could take and return which made their life far easier, and the porters were rapturous.'

Perhaps it is not surprising to discover that Alastair is now a successful manager at a global software firm. The absence of power, permission, budget or resources need not stop you from making an impact. Have the courage to find a better way of doing things.

4. Step up in a crisis

Crises separate leaders from followers. Leaders step up, followers step back. Stepping back is safe: in that moment of crisis and uncertainty you can see which way the wind blows, and then

Crises separate leaders from followers

follow everyone else. In many firms, it is safer to be collectively wrong than to stand up and be right on your own.

Every crisis creates a vacuum, where no one is not quite sure what to do. Someone needs to take the lead. The COVID-19 pandemic was a classic example. In one weekend in March 2020, the world of work was transformed in businesses around the world. Before then, working from home (WFH) was widely ridiculed as being SFH: shirking from home. With a few notable exceptions, no one with serious career aspirations worked from home. By the end of the weekend, WFH had become standard practice. The impossible had become normal, and the changes echo to this day. While few firms have gone fully remote, many firms still accept some form of hybrid working.

It is easy to think that in a crisis the CEO goes into command-and-control mode and sorts the crisis out. That is 20th-century thinking where the Great Man (nearly always a man in the 20th century) could change the fate of the firm, of the nation or the world. The world has changed. It is so complex and volatile that one man, or woman, cannot know the answers to everything. Smart CEOs know that they cannot know everything. COVID-19 exemplified this: no one had ever come across anything like it before. No CEO, however great, could solve the problem of moving a business from being in-person to being remote. This meant that managers everywhere had a chance to step up, find innovative solutions and have significant impact: radical change was needed and expected.

In a crisis, never assume that someone else knows the problem. Don't assume that you have to delegate the problem upwards. In practice, everyone will be delighted to see you taking the initiative and suggesting solutions. Once you suggest a solution, you may well be asked to make it happen: you will be in control and having impact.

Crisis creates the opportunity to step up and have impact

Teach First is a typical example of the challenge and opportunities which the COVID-19 crisis provided. It is now the largest graduate recruiter in the UK. It recruits and trains great graduates to teach in areas of significant disadvantage, which have historically been seen as unattractive places to teach. The training of teachers and teaching itself has always been very high touch: teachers and pupils work together in classrooms. Overnight, that changed. Russell Hobby, then CEO of Teach First, had a decision to make: could the programme go ahead? And if it went ahead, there were endless fundamental questions to resolve:

- How would the trainee teachers be trained? Teachers had never been trained remotely before.

- How would the annual gathering of all the participants work if they could not get together in person?

- How would teaching work without a school to go to?

- How would the trainee teachers be supported and mentored when they could not go into school, they could not meet their pupils in person and they did not have a staffroom to go to for moral support?

Russell knew that he could not answer the questions himself. He had to let go and let each team work out their own answers. In his words:

'I had to get people to ditch the old way of thinking and of doing things. We just had to throw our KPIs (key performance indicators) out of the window. Instead, there are no constraints. Just do your best. And then people would ask me questions like, "What if we miss our retention KPI?" I said I don't care just do your best. Those KPIs and controls were obstacles to success. We just had to think like a greenfield operation where we're doing everything for the first time. As a result, they all found it very exciting. All the hard work was done by a team who just rewrote the entire curriculum to make it work online. Mostly I just got out of their way and left them to own it.

What I was doing was very anti-performance management. I told them, "Don't worry about the performance targets I am not measuring you. Just do what it takes, and we will trust you to do the right thing."'

5. Work on the CEO's agenda

It is tempting to think that the CEO is like the captain of a ship: you turn the wheel, push some buttons and pull a lever and then the ship moves in the direction you have planned for it. That works if you really are a ship's captain. But if you are a CEO, or even a president or prime minister, you make an awkward discovery: you can turn wheels, push buttons and pull levers but nothing very much happens. The wheel, buttons and levers appear not to be connected to anything. And if they are connected to anything, they appear to have a mind of their own and do their own thing. As a CEO you are not dealing with wheels, buttons and levers: you are dealing with people and power.

This is what former Prime Minister Theresa May found out when she served as Home Secretary. She had been trying to get the civil service to prioritise an initiative for months, but it went nowhere. Although she is usually calm and reasonable, she had had enough. She banged her hands on the table and made her displeasure abundantly clear. The startled civil servant replied, 'Oh. . . we didn't realise you were actually serious about this before. . . we can start work on it now. . . '. It is remarkably frustrating to be in charge but not in control. CEOs greatly value team members who both understand and act on their agenda.

For both CEOs and consultants, finding the solution is the easy part of the work. Strategy consulting partners have a rule of thumb that they spend one-third of their time finding the solution, one-third of the time selling the solution to management and one-third of their time selling in their next assignment. Steve Melcher, who ran a large insurance business, saw the same problem from the CEO perspective. After a three-year transformation programme, he reflected that he knew the answer after about three months. For the next 33 months, he spent two-thirds of his time selling the solution to everyone, so that they really understood it and acted on it.

Making change happen is hard work, even for CEOs. This gives you a wonderful opportunity: help the CEO. When you next hear the CEO make the great speech about how change is going to transform the organisation and make everything better, it is very tempting to switch off and just hear 'blah blah blah' while you think about more important matters, such as the coffee break. That is what most people do: they do not think that the CEO agenda is something that they can really act on. But if you can act on it, you have the potential to make a real impact and to make a powerful friend: the CEO.

For instance, David Stephen was running risk for NatWest, then RBS. After the Great Financial Crisis, many people hated bankers. So who do the bankers hate? They hate the risk managers who stop them doing stupid things that could bankrupt the bank in two years' time, but will earn bankers their bonuses this year. Being a risk manager at a bank is not the high road to popularity; even the CEO sees you as a nuisance to be tolerated. The CEO decided that his big new idea was to become the most customer-focused bank, anywhere.

What has customer focus got to do with risk? Risk is in the bowels of the bank, doing risk analysis, managing risk processes and stopping stupid stuff happening. David thought differently. He decided to spend at least one day a month in branches, seeing how risk affected front line operations. He quickly discovered how some processes were redundant, some were defective, some impaired customer service and how some risk was not being managed properly. This knowledge transformed his relationship with the CEO for two reasons. First, he was able to bring information from the front line, which no reporting system will ever pick up: he was bringing the view from the bottom of the mountain to the top of the mountain. Second, he was talking to the CEO about his agenda and his priorities: customer focus.

Manage your work portfolio

Working on the right agenda is vital for your career, but comes with a health warning for your career as well. If you only work on your big and exciting agenda, you will fail: you still need to perform well with the routine of your day job, and you still need to do your fair share of non-promotable and voluntary work which all organisations depend on. In practice you need to build a balanced portfolio of work which has four types of work:

Build a balanced portfolio of work

1 *Making an impact.* This is your big agenda, and it is promotable work. It will have visibility across the organisation and will have impact beyond your own area of responsibility.

2 *Performing your day job.* This is your routine but necessary work: preparing reports, doing admin, and doing the day-to-day tasks

of your job. If you don't do this, you fail. If you do it well, you keep your job but you will not be making a special impact and you will not stand out relative to your peers.

3 *Providing support*, to others and to the firm. This can range from taking part in interview panels to leading internal workshops, to mentoring new staff, to organising the leaving party for a colleague. It is about being a good corporate citizen. Some firms recognise this, others don't.

4 *Investing in yourself.* Self-improvement is not just about formal training. it is also about making sure you get the right experiences to stretch and develop yourself. Making an impact is a good way to stretch and develop yourself.

The balance of your work portfolio will shift over time. At some times of year, performing your day job may take all of your time; other times you will be able to take more initiative and create your own agenda. At the start of the year, think about what a balanced work portfolio looks like for you, and then take stock of your work portfolio from time to time.

Summary

By now, you will have made all the essential investments in achieving impact: you will be the colleague of choice, you will have a web of trusted allies across the firm and you will be working on the right agenda. Now you have to convert all this potential into reality. You have to make it happen, which is the focus of the next and subsequent chapters.

chapter 4

Make it happen

Reliability is one of the top five expectations that managers have of each team member, along with hard work, proactivity, intelligence and ambition. Just 61 per cent of managers say that they are satisfied with the reliability of their team members.

There are two reasons why managers feel let down by the reliability of team members. The first is that some people are simply unreliable. Here is a classic view from a senior executive who runs a highly qualified global team which has more degrees than team members:

> I see too many people who can't deliver, can't communicate, and get frustrated. Many simply do not deliver on time. They will say something will be delivered on Monday and then I have to send them a reminder on Wednesday saying where is it? It is not good enough to deliver 70 or 80 per cent of the time. If you say you are going to deliver on a certain day, you have to deliver on that day.

That probably sounds familiar: we all get let down more often than we would wish.

We all get let down more often than we would wish

The second reason is that managers became managers because they succeeded in their previous role: they had higher standards and higher performance than their peers. That causes problems when they get promoted, because they think that everyone should live up to the exceptional standards they displayed. It was a learning process Maddy Storr went through when she started her rapid rise through the management ranks of a global firm:

> I was a rubbish leader to start with. My bar is set very high and I found that no one can meet it. I had an epiphany when I realised that people don't have the same standards, commitment or drive that I do. But they may have better ideas. So I have to adjust my expectations. I still keep raising the bar, but I do not set it impossibly high.

If you want to succeed, you have to be reliable and you have to deliver 100 per cent of the time. You will not be remembered for the

99 times you delivered on time; you will be remembered for the one time you were perceived to not deliver.

Personal productivity matters. In a world of give and take, you have to give as well as take. You have to deliver on your commitments and support others

---

'Get s**t done'

---

if you want them to support you. As many executives put it to me, both in interviews and in workshops, you have to 'get s**t done'. Cade Tan, a Singaporean executive who has worked across advertising, banking and now technology, expressed it simply. She said:

> **The key to success is an immense amount of hard work, a deep sense of accountability and bringing a sense of humour to any difficult situation. I am meticulous and have strived to do better than others. I might not be the smartest person in the room, but I try my best to 'Get Shit Done'.**

If you complete tasks reliably, consistently and to a high standard, you will stand out from your peers, however well qualified they may appear to be.

Productivity is both a skill set and a mindset. Much has been written about productivity tools and techniques, which will be briefly summarised below. But none of these tools and techniques work without the productivity mindset; and if you have the productivity mindset, you probably will not need to rely on any productivity hacks. So we will start with the productivity mindset and then look at the skills of productivity.

The productivity mindset: own your work

There are always excuses why you cannot do something:

- feeling tired or stressed;
- being overwhelmed by the complexity or volume of work you face;

- lacking the power or resources to do what you need to do;
- having uncertainty about goals, choices, direction and outcomes;
- being distracted by the joys of social media, internet, shopping, holiday planning;
- being distracted by colleagues' gossip or requests;
- falling victim to the fatal attraction of the coffee machine and fridge;
- dealing with too many other urgent and important priorities.

High-impact managers are productive not because they all have some secret productivity tool or skill set. They have a secret mindset, which is consistent among all of them: they own their work.

If you are doing dull work on behalf of someone else, it is hard to feel motivated. On the other hand, if you are doing something which is important to you, you will find a way of making it happen. High-impact managers act like it is their own business. They act like owners, not hired hands. When you own your own business, you think and act differently:

- Make every minute count just as much as every penny counts.
- Find ways to make things happen and deal with obstacles.
- Stay focused on the goal, which removes any doubt and confusion about what to do.
- Deal with the routine noise of work ruthlessly, to create enough time to focus on achieving your goal.
- Act with urgency and authority, not like a disempowered and demoralised hired hand.
- Ignore all the distractions of social media, colleagues and coffee.

You can own your work, even if you do not own the firm. The key is to find the right agenda. If you create an agenda which matters to you, excites you and you believe in, you will own your agenda and own your work. We have

Own your work, even if you do not own the firm

already seen that crafting the right agenda determines your ability to have impact; it also drives your productivity.

A model of productivity

Mike Elliott runs a team of 350 people spread across 19 countries around the world. His approach is typical of productive managers and it may, or may not, work for you. What matters is finding similar clarity about how you can stay at your productive peak:

'My most productive time is in the morning. I will often use the Pomodoro approach to crunch through something quickly in the morning or to give myself a jolt to get things moving when my energy is low after lunch. I use the Eisenhower Matrix every day. It is a two-by-two grid which maps out what is important and what is urgent that I need to deal with on that day. I like to get some easy things done at the start of the day to get things going and build momentum. Then I review my progress at the end of the day to see what I have done and what more has blown in.

There are things I do to get things done. I believe in one-touch emails: only touch each email once to avoid procrastination. I find a quick walk outdoors will help me regain my energy. I have a calendar which all my colleagues can see and they can put meetings into my diary. To avoid overload, I block out certain times as focus time which is reserved for me and they cannot put in appointments. That means that if anything urgent arises I still have some time to deal with it.'

The seven habits of productivity

The productivity mindset is a vital start. Having some basic productivity disciplines ensures that you 'get s**t done' consistently and effectively.

1. Set clear goals

Be clear about what you want to achieve this year, month, week, day and hour. Naturally, other matters will come up that you have to deal with. This is the noise of organisational life. It is easy to lose yourself in the noise of reacting to demands. You need clear goals so that you can stay focused on the signal, not the noise: be clear about what you must achieve.

Executives with the clearest goals are often the best at dealing with the trivia of work. They are so focused on achieving their goal that they do not let trivia stand in their way. They just deal with it rather than worrying about it or putting it off. The old saying, 'If you want something done, ask a busy person' rings true. The busier you are, the less time you have to waste, so you just do it.

In practice, work expands or contracts to the time available. With plenty of time, it is possible to spend all day worrying about writing a routine letter and working out the logistics of stamps, printers, envelopes and

> **Work expands or contracts to the time available**

addresses. If you are busy, then dealing with 30 emails is simply a minor irritation which you fit in between dealing with more important matters.

2. Break big tasks into small tasks

A large task can feel overwhelming. Often it is not clear where you can start or how you can do it: the result is procrastination and worry. The solution is to plan your work so that you break your work down into small chunks. For instance, researching and writing a book is a huge task. Good planning means breaking the book down into chapters, then breaking each chapter down into sections, and then focusing on writing 500 words at a time. Anyone can write 500 words. If the plan is good, then write 500 words 120 times and you complete a 60,000-word book. The value of the book is for you to decide.

3. Work in sprints

You cannot sustain high-intensity work all day. This was discovered by the godfather of time and motion studies, FW Taylor, in his book, *The Principles of Scientific Management*, published in 1911. Taylor's goal was to wring every last ounce of productivity out of workers. He was not on the side of workers. The workers' unions hated both him and scientific management. Despite this, one of his insights was that workers should rest for at least five minutes in every hour even if they did not feel tired. He found that each rest break increased their productivity greatly: it was better to have 55 productive minutes than 60 unproductive minutes every hour. Rest is not for wimps; it is for productivity. A quick coffee or walk around the office is a good rest: you do not need to sleep at your hot desk.

Rest is not for wimps; it is for productivity

Thinking work, as opposed to manual work, may well require more regular breaks. If you have high concentration work, you may only be able to maintain quality for 40 minutes, or even less. That is fine. Set yourself a target for the next 40 minutes and then go for it. This is sometimes called the Pomodoro Technique after a kitsch kitchen timer shaped like a tomato (*pomodoro*, in Italian). Whether you choose to use a timer in the shape of a tomato is up to you.

4. Reward yourself

St Augustine's prayer of 'make me virtuous. . . but not just yet' could be the prayer of all office workers. We want to be virtuous and work, but the contest between the attractions of work versus the attractions of the fridge, social media or the coffee machine is an unequal one. You need a way of avoiding temptation. You can do this by turning St Augustine's prayer around: 'make me a sinner. . . but not just yet'. Allow yourself to give in to the temptation of the fridge, coffee machine or social media. . . but not just yet. Let yourself indulge, briefly, as a reward for completing a short sprint of work. This gives you an incentive to stay focused. It also gives you the chance to refresh and refocus at regular intervals.

Don't punish yourself by denying yourself the sins of social media, coffee and relaxation. Instead, make them your reward for doing some good work.

5. Avoid interruptions

Distractions destroy productivity. A study of coders found that each distraction cost them 15 minutes of lost time, and that they became more error prone after the distraction. That

> **Distractions destroy productivity**

means if colleagues drop by just twice an hour with a social question such as 'would you like a coffee?' or 'did you see the game last night?', that is half the day lost to interruptions.

At the office, it is hard to avoid interruptions. In theory, your home should be a more controlled environment where you can do your high concentration work. This means you have to avoid the distraction of the fridge, the lure of social media and the demands of the dog wanting a walk. If you work at home, create proper boundaries between work and home life.

6. Find your rhythm

Some people are better in the mornings, others in the afternoons. Some people like to do routine work in the morning to create a sense of progress and leave the more challenging work to the afternoon; others prefer to get stuck in important matters first and deal with routine matters at the end of the day. There is only one perfect solution: the solution which works for you. See the earlier box ('A model of productivity') for a classic example.

Part of your rhythm should include some unscheduled time, because the unexpected always happens. If you are 100 per cent time committed, you have no capacity to respond to unexpected opportunities, crises, meetings or requests. In the unlikely event that the unexpected does not happen, the unscheduled time gives you the chance to catch up on all the things you meant to do, but did not have the time to do.

You can only control your rhythm if you control your diary. Professionals find this hard because they like to please. When a colleague or client asks for a meeting, the natural instinct is to say 'yes'. If you always say yes, you lose control, lose your rhythm and lose your productivity. The alternative to 'yes' is not always 'no'. The better alternative is to negotiate a more suitable time. If it is a large group meeting, this is not possible. But many smaller meetings can be scheduled flexibly. Use that flexibility to arrange a time which allows you to keep your rhythm and stay productive.

Your rhythm includes where you work as well as when you work. Be clear about where you do what sort of work best. Typically, high concentration work is done best where you face no interruptions. This can either be at home or in a closed office, if you are doing things like writing code, preparing a presentation or analysing data. If your work is more about communication, creativity, building trust, persuading or problem solving, you need to be with your colleagues: the office is usually better for this than trying to work remotely.

7. Maintain boundaries

The statistics show that the average working year is shorter than it has ever been. Statistics and averages can be very misleading. The chances are that if you are reading this book, you are not an average worker: you are probably working much more than average. And even when you leave work, work never leaves you: the electronic shackles of email, instant messaging and the internet mean that you never fully switch off. The boundaries between work and home have become blurred, even more so with the advent of WFH.

Even when you leave work, work never leaves you

You need to create boundaries so that you can recharge your batteries properly. For instance, one recent graduate in a flat share has a routine where she walks to the local coffee shop in the morning to grab a coffee. When she returns, mentally she returns not to her flat but to her work. Her room is ready with her special work mat set out. In the evening, she reverses the walk and comes back to her home and her work mat and all her work materials have been put away. She has, inadvertently, discovered the joys of the commute which separate home and office. Creating these boundaries helps with both productivity and work–life balance.

Summary

Being personally productive gives you the credibility and permission to take on discretionary tasks, start new initiatives and take some risk. You can start to make the agenda, not take the agenda. But to make the agenda, you must convert your personal support into specific support for your idea. You need to discover the subtle art of selling, without appearing to sell. That is the focus of the next chapter.

chapter 5

Sell, sell, sell (without selling)

To have impact, you have to persuade colleagues and clients to do things. But few people like selling or being sold to. You have to learn the art of selling, without being seen to sell.

The great sales challenge

No one likes to be called a salesperson. Even salespeople prefer to be called something else, like account executive, relationship manager or partner in a professional services firm. But the reality is that the more senior you become, the more you become a salesperson. You will not be selling second-hand cars or double-glazing. Instead, you will be selling your ideas, your agenda, your priorities. You will be selling to show that your department's needs are more worthy than those of other departments that are competing for the same limited amount of budget and management support. You will be competing to prove to your clients that your services are preferable to those of your competition. If you cannot sell your ideas, you fail.

> **The more senior you become, the more you become a salesperson**

> **If you cannot sell your ideas, you fail**

At junior levels, you rarely have to sell anything because work is handed to you. You do not choose your agenda, the agenda chooses you. As you progress through the organisation you shift from taking the agenda to making the agenda. You have to start persuading colleagues and possibly clients that you have the right idea, right solution, right agenda.

Your changing role is captured by the way that professional services firms are informally organised into three levels of ascending seniority:

- grinders
- minders
- finders.

Here is what grinders, minders and finders do:

- *Grinders* are the entry-level associates who do all the grunt work: reviewing legal documents, doing research, preparing presentations, checking data and facts. If you do this well, you are promoted to manager, where you require a completely different set of skills.

- *Minders* manage the work of the grinders, and may well start to manage some client relationships. Managing work is very different from doing work. As a result, many grinders do not become good minders and they wash out of the organisation before reaching Valhalla for anyone in professional services: becoming a partner.

- *Finders* are partners, and their performance is assessed on how much revenue they generate for the firm. Each finder is responsible for many hungry mouths which need to be fed with project work. The very smooth and polished partner sitting in front of you is, in reality, a salesperson.

The great sales challenge is even greater because your colleagues do not want you to act like a salesperson. In most cultures, if you are pushy and overtly selling your ideas and your priorities, your efforts will backfire on you. You will look like you are being very selfish in promoting yourself and your ideas; you will not be seen to be a team player.

Selling within your organisation turns out to be very different from classic sales techniques. You do not need to master the art of 16 different sorts of close; you do not need to pump yourself up by attending a sales convention where you will be urged to 'Close that Sale!' You have to master a very different art form: the art of selling without appearing to sell.

Fortunately, you have probably already spent a lifetime practising the art of selling without selling: the art is called persuasion. We spend our lives trying to persuade people to do things, from persuading toddlers to eat their greens to persuading colleagues to support us.

At work you are involved in hard-form persuasion. You do not just want to persuade people that you have a smart idea. Your form of persuasion has to lead to a practical outcome: a colleague has to do something you want them to do, or they have to approve something or help you in some way.

The art of persuading colleagues to do things for you can be quite sophisticated, but it can also be very simple. At its simplest, you have to ask the question; if you don't ask the question, you

If you don't ask the question, you don't get the answer

don't get the answer. This is obvious but, as George Orwell wrote: 'to see what is in front of one's nose needs a constant struggle'. If you don't ask the question, you guarantee that you will not get the answer you need. If you ask the question, you at least give yourself a chance. It may even help you achieve the impossible: joining the Emperor of Japan's tennis club as a foreigner (see the box below).

How to join the Emperor's tennis club

Richard Grabinger is an executive at Hitachi. At age 16 he had an inoperable head tumour and was given two weeks to live. He had a 1 in 100 chance of surviving. He survived against all odds with an experimental treatment and now makes the most of every year: he lives each year as if it is his last. It gives him energy, motivation and focus which is hard to match in sports and business. He is very much into all kinds of sports and is a keen tennis player.

He was working in Tokyo as an expat, and he wanted to join a local tennis club. He saw a club from his apartment in Hiro, a nice neighbourhood in Tokyo. He did not know that it was very exclusive and used by the old emperor and that there is an up to 20-year waiting list: you and your family have to be thoroughly vetted, and your tennis skills have to be assessed. It is famously difficult for the Japanese to join, so what chance does a *gaijin* (foreigner) have at such a place?

Richard takes up the story: 'I did not know how hard it was to join. I just saw the club from my apartment, and I walked in. I walked past all the signs saying "members only" and went to the reception and said, "Can I join the club?" Within six months I had become a member patiently following the process and all rules and requirements. I did not realise it at the time, but they reserve a small percentage of their membership for suitable foreigners. They realise that foreigners who dare to request to join the club mostly are expats or ambassadors who have a time stamp on them and a several years' waiting list will not work for them.

If you don't ask the question, you don't get the answer. Maybe I got lucky but you have to make your own luck.'

If in doubt, ask the question. That sounds easy, but it is not easy for rational and emotional reasons. The emotional reason is that we fear rejection and embarrassment. The rational reason is that it is not always clear what question you should ask, to whom and when. Ask the wrong question to the wrong person at the wrong time and you guarantee rejection, which makes your task far harder.

If in doubt, ask the question

The art of persuasion in an organisation is rarely about asking one person one question once, unless it is a very simple request. Instead, you are slowly building consensus. You are crafting a story and you are helping your colleagues be part of that story.

You are not telling and selling a story you already have: you are inviting colleagues to help craft the story with you. This is central to selling your idea without selling: do not attempt to push your idea down their throats and into their heads. They will, rightly, want to resist. Instead, let them feel that they have been part of creating the story. This gives your colleagues a sense of ownership over the story that emerges. Very few people choose to argue against their own story or their own idea.

Very few people choose to argue against their own story

To reinforce the point: the worst way to persuade the organisation is to try and sell your brilliant, fully formed idea to everyone. No one will have any ownership over it. If you are the CEO and have sufficient power, you can force your idea on everyone. But even then, you will only gain compliance. You will not gain the sort of commitment that you need where colleagues will improve your idea, overcome problems for you and put in the discretionary effort that turns an average idea into a great idea.

Persuading after the event sounds like an obvious error, but it is one which many CEOs make. They come up with some great new transformational idea, possibly with the help of consultants. After months of working up their idea, they announce it with great fanfare at a corporate event, and then wonder why no one seems very enthusiastic beyond their immediate circle of executives who have been involved in planning the new direction. There are at least three problems with this 'tell and sell' approach to persuasion:

- No one has ownership over the idea: they feel no sense of agency and no commitment. It is hard to be enthusiastic about someone else's idea.

- Managers see CEOs and ideas come and go. They learn how to survive each new regime. Often the easiest path to survival is to do nothing: wait and see what needs to be done, when. Doing nothing also happens to be a good way to kill initiatives: if no one does anything, by definition nothing happens and the idea dies. You need active support, not passive compliance, for an idea to take flight.

- No one will understand what the great idea means for them personally. The CEO will have spent months working out all the advantages and disadvantages and options. It is impossible to communicate all that detail in a 40-minute event, even with Q&A.

Managers below CEO level do not have the luxury of formal power: you cannot force your ideas on the organisation. You have to build active commitment, not passive compliance. That means your selling process does not start after you have crafted your idea. You start persuading and selling from the moment you first have your half-formed idea. Think of your idea as a story, and craft that story with your colleagues.

Crafting a story with your colleagues is a natural five-step process:

1 Define your big idea.

2 Make your case: rational, political and emotional.

3 Build your coalition: ask for advice.

4 Deal with objections.

5 Confirm agreement in private, then in public.

Think of each step as a set of traffic lights: do not jump the lights because that will cause you problems. If all the lights are set to green, go straight ahead and do not pause at each step. Make it as easy for yourself as possible.

Just do it

There is a radical alternative to this five-step approach to persuasion: just do it. It is always easier to ask forgiveness after the event than it is to ask for permission before the event. This is how many of the cases presented so far started:

- Hospital porters reorganised the wheelchairs in the hospital: asking for permission would have gone nowhere fast. They just did it; it worked and it was accepted.

- The Google apprenticeship programme started under the radar: Amanda Timberg set up an internal website that became the definitive resource. The website created the momentum and credibility for a global programme.

- Nancy De Vore took on the UNGA programme for Salesforce because no one else would touch it: no permission needed.

'Act first, talk later' is very powerful. You quickly learn what works and what does not work. If it succeeds, you build momentum and everyone wants to join your bandwagon. If it does not work, you can quietly redirect your efforts elsewhere:

➤

> you will only have lost some of your discretionary time and effort.
>
> If you act first and talk later, do not ignore your day job. Meeting your regular targets gives you all the permission you need to innovate, try new things and have more impact.

Here is how the five steps of persuasion work:

1. Define your big idea

Your idea has to be very, very simple. Your colleagues have many things to worry about. Your agenda is important to you, but not so important to them.

Your idea has to be very, very simple

You have to show that your idea is worth their time. Working on the right idea will help you:

- gain access to colleagues who may be hard to reach: they will understand why they need to talk with you;
- overcome objections and obstacles: if the goal is big and bold enough, it is worth overcoming the inevitable challenges any big idea faces;
- sustain your personal motivation to make it happen.

Your idea has to be as simple as the headline you will see on a newspaper or a website. We have already encountered big ideas which can be summarised very simply:

- 'Organise an expedition across the Empty Quarter of Arabia.'
- 'Develop a global apprenticeship programme.'
- 'Achieve corporate impact at the UN General Assembly.'

In each case, the successful idea had three vital characteristics. It was:

- *Big and clear enough to gain attention and support from key stakeholders*: crossing the Empty Quarter was presented as an opportunity for the governments of Oman, Saudi Arabia and Qatar. As you think about your idea, be very clear about who it is going to help and why. Clarity about the benefits of your idea is the lifeblood which will sustain it.

- *Very simple to state*. It was as short as a newspaper headline, so everyone could remember it. As with a newspaper headline, the detail was left unstated. That is how it should be. You fill in the detail with your colleagues later: that is the art of story crafting.

- *Unclear about how it was going to happen*. When the high-impact managers started out with their ideas, no one knew how it would work. This allowed the managers to progress to the first real stage of persuasion, which was to ask for advice: they could build support by building ownership of the challenge across all the relevant stakeholders. Sometimes, vagueness can be your friend and detail can be your enemy. Invite your colleagues to help you fill in the blanks, rather than dictating an answer to them that they will not own.

2. Make your case: rational, emotional and political

I first discovered that selling is not entirely rational when I was selling dishwashing liquid in the north of Scotland. As I went round housing estates, I noticed that many houses proudly displayed a bottle of Fairy Liquid in their kitchen window, above the sink. No other brand of dishwashing liquid could be seen anywhere. At first, I thought this might be some modern Scottish tradition to add to haggis, kilts and tossing the caber. I then discovered the truth.

Fairy Liquid is not just the brand leader, it is the premium and upmarket brand. The advertising constantly but subtly reinforces this through the choice of hands and dishes that feature. If you want to prove that you are house proud, spending a few pennies extra on Fairy Liquid is a cheap way to do it, and you can show your neighbours that you never settle for second best. If you prefer to economise and you are prepared to settle for second best, you do not advertise the fact. You hide your cheap bottle of dishwashing liquid beneath the kitchen sink.

If dishwashing liquid is an emotional decision, any decision can be an emotional decision. Humans are not always entirely rational. Put them in an organisation, they become political animals as well. So when you make your case, it

Humans are not always entirely rational

has to work rationally, emotionally and politically. It is not enough to have a great idea and wait for the world to recognise its brilliance: you will have a very long wait.

If you want to make your case, the obvious starting point is to make a strong rational case for it. The problem is that rational cases are often contested, for good reasons and less good reasons:

- Everyone knows that the spreadsheet has been constructed from the bottom right-hand corner back: start with the desired answer and tweak the assumptions until the right number (plus a bit for safety) miraculously appears.

- PowerPoint presentations are good for sharing information and ideas, less good for persuading. When did you last see two heads of government trying to persuade each other with competing PowerPoint presentations?

- Your rational case may look good to you, but how does it affect colleagues elsewhere? More support and resource for your idea may mean less support for their idea; or perhaps your idea will cause them more work; or more senior colleagues may feel upstaged by you.

Making your rational case

Textbooks and business schools teach you how to find the most compelling evidence to make your case. But evidence is only half of the rational case. The other half is how you choose to present your rational case.

For a moment, try to recall the details of the last spreadsheet someone presented at a meeting. Few people can do this, unless you happen to be an actuary. Now try to recall a story that one of your colleagues told you recently. The chances are that you can recall at least some of the story: you will recall the headlines, even if you cannot recall the details. So how will your colleagues remember your pitch: will they remember the spreadsheet that you spent hours crafting, or will they remember the headlines of a story you told them?

Numbers and stories would appear to go together as naturally as an octopus in a tree. But this is where you can put data visualisation to good use. This was part of Florence Nightingale's secret of success. She is best known for having created modern nursing,

> **Numbers and stories would appear to go together as naturally as an octopus in a tree**

during the Crimean War of 1853 to 1856. But she was also a statistician who knew how to make statistics tell a story. She created the polar area diagram, which is the precursor to today's histograms and other sorts of data visualisation (Figure 5.1). It was a very powerful way of showing, in graphic terms, that far more soldiers were dying of disease and infection than were dying from enemy action. The picture told a story, and it was powerful enough that the government of the day backed her ideas on improving hospital care in the field. A picture told a story which the data alone could not tell. Partly as a result, modern nursing was born.

Never underestimate the power of a story which is relevant to the people you want to persuade. Nightingale's interest was improved hospital care; the government's interest was in winning the war. She focused on solving the government's problem: they were losing far too many soldiers, and they did not realise that most of the deaths were unnecessary. She achieved her goal by focusing on the government's goal. Like the best 21st-century leaders she made things happen through people she did not control.

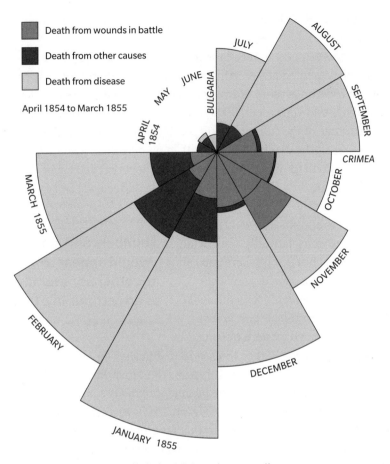

Figure 5.1 Florence Nightingale's polar area diagram

There is an alternative to persuading through numbers: use the voice of the customer. It is easy to argue over numbers, but much harder to argue over the voice of the customer. If the customer says something or does something, that is reality. Even if you think the customer is wrong, you cannot deny what they say and how they act. If cash is king, the customer is queen: do not argue with the customer. The customer can be your best ally in making your case.

> **Cash is king, the customer is queen**

Using the customer to make your case is routine in market-facing firms like P&G and Unilever: they track market share, competitive positioning and customer attitudes and behaviour relentlessly. Using the voice of the customer is even more effective in less market-facing departments and firms, because it is so unusual: you bring a different perspective which is very hard for anyone to argue against.

By bringing the voice of the customer into your firm, you add value. You bring new information and new insight. You do not need to arrange expensive market research to discover the voice of the customer. All you have to do is to talk to a few customers directly: most of them are delighted to talk openly about their experience of dealing with your firm.

The example of Google illustrates the persuasive impact of bringing the voice of the customer into the firm.

Let the customer make your rational case for you

Google is very much an engineering lead company. At one of its sites, there is an A4 sheet of paper above each urinal which reminds engineers how to spot and debug errors in code. The message is clear: whatever you do, do not stop thinking about the product. Typically, engineers push out product and see if it works. It is an approach which has worked with great success for many years.

Tia Lendo was head of K12 education marketing at Google. Her challenge was to get the Chromebook adopted by schools, where Apple has historically had a very strong presence. That meant helping engineers understand how to adapt the Chromebook to make it more attractive for schools, and persuading schools to adopt the Chromebook. Tia's insight was that she was not the best person to persuade either engineers or customers. Schools would be most effective at converting both the engineers and other schools. She organised schools to do the persuading for her.

➤

Google already had a teacher academy, which they used to get feedback on the Chromebook and other products. This was her vehicle for learning and persuading. Some changes were immediately needed, like a more robust keyboard for small but clumsy fingers. But the real value was in discovering how schools could really benefit from Chromebooks. Because the Chromebook is web based, it is much easier to administer: IT managers could administer the school's entire fleet of Chromebooks (updates, restricted access to certain websites) without ever actually having to touch the kit. Teachers could see in real time how pupils were tackling problems, and could give real time feedback.

In her words: 'At first, we were just learning what worked and what the teachers really wanted and how they could best use the Chromebook. So for the first year or so we were just working with 30 schools or so. Then we got them to share with all of their networks and very quickly the Google Chromebook became the number one product for K to 12 schools in the United States, and then globally within five years.'

Making your emotional case

What has emotion got to do with business? Everything.

Florence Nightingale understood the power of emotion. She played the media well and the *Times* started to portray her as 'The Lady with the Lamp', spreading her care and compassion to wounded soldiers in Crimea. For sentimental Victorians, this made her beyond reproach: they might argue against her innovative polar area diagram, but only a cad and a bounder would argue against The Lady with the Lamp.

To understand the value of rational versus emotional persuasion, spend an evening at home watching some shows. But instead of focusing on the shows, focus on the advertising during the breaks. Some advertising will focus on a rational argument, especially when there is a sale on. But much of the advertising reaches beyond rational arguments. For instance, car buying should perhaps be a rational purchase where you weigh up different advantages such as safety, capacity, fuel usage and range, and cost of ownership. In practice, not much advertising focuses on such benefits. Instead, advertising focuses on the lifestyle of the buyer: the buyer of a Tesla Cybertruck is likely to be very different from the buyer of a Honda CR-V, aimed at families. Automakers know that you are not just buying a car; you are buying an identity.

You are not just buying a car; you are buying an identity

The importance of emotion in consumer buying decisions is well understood by advertising agencies. But consumers are also your colleagues. They do not suddenly cease to be human when they walk past reception. All that changes is that they are expected to behave more logically and rationally, but they are still human. They still have hopes, fears and dreams. Ignore human nature at your peril.

For instance, Steve Cutts was tasked with finding cost savings at the UN where he was assistant secretary-general. That should be a relatively rational task. He picks up the story: 'The office was full of private offices and cubicles which did not work. The cubicles fail to give the privacy which many conversations needed and they also prevented the collaboration that happens when you have a fully open plan office. And moving to more flexible working would save at least $50 million a year, which was much more than the one-off cost of around $37 million required to refit the offices.'

His proposed re-organisation was a no brainer: save $50 million a year, improve collaboration and improve privacy when it is needed. The United Nations is full of very smart people who understand logic and reason. What could possibly go wrong?

The logic was impeccable, but it failed to deal with human nature. Humans are territorial and they did not want to give up their territory, even if it was only a cubicle. At least they could decorate it and mark it out as their own space. Steve was proposing to make everyone homeless at the office. The result was a letter from 18 under-secretaries-general (USGs) vehemently objecting to his plans and giving all sorts of plausible rational reasons for why moving to open plan would be a disaster.

The usual reaction to such a challenge would be to double down on the rational case, but that would simply entrench the opposition. One assistant secretary-general will not win against 18 USGs, however good the case may be. Instead, Steve went into listening mode. He met each USG personally and held town hall meetings with all staff to discuss the proposals. By listening he not only showed that he respected them, he was also able to modify the plans to meet most of their needs while achieving the cost savings.

Spot the motivation: emotional

Once you can tap into real motivation, good things happen. People want to support you and want to help you. You cease to be a salesperson trying to force your idea on a colleague. You become their partner of choice because you are giving them something they want. Vikas Pota, founder of T4 Education, found out about the power of tapping into people's needs during the pandemic.

Vikas saw that teachers globally were struggling with the same issues about how to teach remotely. So he put a call together to let teachers share experience, expecting 20–30 people to turn up. Two hundred and fifty attended the first call, and he realised that he was meeting an unmet need. Attendees all the way from Australia to Africa to Chile and beyond were asking the same question: 'what does the new normal look like?'

Vikas realised that the need was not about rational answers and more content: it was about connection in a world where teachers had become disconnected. The best rational answers probably already existed in a policy manual or on the internet somewhere. But the most credible answers which teachers could relate to came from their peers. Peer-to-peer exchanges are a game changer because they build a sense of community, they create connection and offer up credible solutions from lived experience.

With that first call in April 2020, Vikas had tapped into a real need. By the time of the next call a month later, 103,000 teachers had logged in, even from beneath trees in Sierra Leone and from mountains in Bhutan. If Vikas had been selling content, few people would have turned up. By answering a human need for connection and being part of something bigger than yourself, he created a community. That community has now blossomed into 200,000 teachers globally; T4 Education listed on NASDAQ in 2022 and has inaugurated the World's Best School Prize which gets the support of presidents and prime ministers around the world.

Vikas's success did not come from building a rational business case. It came from building a community and meeting a human need.

Making your political case

Ignore politics at your peril. In the words of author and expert on office politics Niven Postma: 'If you don't do politics, politics will do you'. All organisations are political because there is a constant contest for resources, support, ideas, budget and personal promotion. Making your political case is not about preparing a presentation or working up a spreadsheet. It is about building a coalition in support of your idea. That means you have to understand the motivations of all the different experts and power brokers who you need on your side.

> 'If you don't do politics, politics will do you'

Once again, Florence Nightingale lights the way. Although she built a strong rational case (the polar area diagrams) and a strong emotional case (the Lady with the Lamp) she knew that was not enough. She realised that the military establishment might well oppose her: they did not like females near wars (except for all the wrong reasons), and they certainly did not want an amateur interfering in their business. In the words of Sir John Hall, the chief British Army medical officer in Crimea: 'Miss Nightingale shows an ambitious struggling after power inimical to the true interests of the medical department.' If you want to make an impact, you will upset people: the bigger the impact, the more the opposition. You cannot fight opposition alone: you need allies.

Florence Nightingale understood the need for political support. She had befriended Sydney Herbert on his honeymoon in Italy. This was fortuitous because he became secretary of war during the Crimean War and acted as her sponsor. At the time, women were not allowed to vote or sit in Parliament: she needed her voice to be heard. Herbert was her sponsor who would be rooting for her when she could not be in the room.

The case of Nightingale and Herbert illustrates once again the importance of having a sponsor who can help smooth the way for you and remove political obstacles.

In addition to your sponsor, your coalition of support will consist of four different types of decision maker. If you have woven your web of support properly (see Chapter 2), you will be well placed to gain the political support you need for your project or idea. A good test of whether you have a supportive relationship with these decision makers is how positively they communicate with you: do they always respond positively to your emails and messages? Do they proactively reach out to you with useful intelligence about opportunities and threats? Are they prepared to spend time with you socially? Here are the four sorts of decision makers you need on board.

1 *Authoriser*: normally there is only one authoriser, who might be the CEO or another senior executive. But the authoriser will want to make sure that the other stakeholders also support the decision.

2 *Users*: these are the people that are going to have to live with the consequences of the decision, and perhaps implement it.

3 *Technical buyers*: they do not have the power to approve your idea, but they can veto it if your idea is not compliant with their rules and processes. You will find technical buyers in finance, legal, health and safety, HR, risk and elsewhere.

4 *Influencers*: they have no formal role in decision making, but will influence the other sorts of buyers with their thinking. Consultants, for instance, have no decision-making authority but will shape the thinking of senior management. You may like them or dislike them, but they are worth having on your side. The voice of the customer can also be very influential in supporting your story.

This coalition building is not exceptional; it is standard practice if you want to make anything worthwhile happen. For instance, launching a new promotional campaign for a detergent is routine: many detergents work on a regular cycle of annual promotions. Each promotion involves an in-store sales campaign with major retailers, supported by increased media spending and possibly by some refreshed advertising. Although routine, it requires building a wide coalition of support:

- *Authoriser*: The marketing director who has the final say but otherwise has minimal involvement. If the director is responsible for 12 brands each of which have four annual promotions, that is 48 approvals for the director to make. There will be many other things the marketing director will be focused on, such as new product development and test markets. Sheer volume of work means that your proposal will not gain much attention, and the marketing director will want to make sure that everyone else supports your promotional idea.

- *Users*: the sales department will be responsible for putting your promotion into practice: they will have to sell it into the retail trade. As a result, they will have strong opinions about what will and will not work with their retail accounts. You need their active support.

- *Technical buyers* make sure your promotion meets all the firm's requirements. You will need to gain approval from (among others):
  - finance, to make sure the budget is correct;
  - manufacturing, to confirm that they can produce the right promotional pack in the right volumes at the right time;
  - design, to produce the desired design for the promotional packaging;
  - legal, to ensure you meet all regulatory requirements and that you are not incurring any unintended liability with your promotion;
  - media, to confirm that the advertising budget is correct and that they can deliver the required media impact at the right time.
- *Influencers* are often the hardest to spot, but can be vital. In this case, the advertising agency may well have views on whether your promotion is in line with the brand strategy. As an external agency, they have no formal say in the decision-making process, but their support or opposition could well make the difference between success and failure. Similarly, the major retail accounts have no say in the decision-making process, but will make or break your promotion in the marketplace. If they do not back your promotion, it will fail.

Spot the motivation: political

The board meeting was what all board meetings are like: a mix of routine and one or two big decisions. The big decisions had already been agreed on in private but needed public confirmation at the board meeting. At the end of it the real discussions happened as everyone milled around the coffee machine.

We had invited a civil servant to attend our board meetings. We needed an inside track about what the department was thinking about our programme. The civil servant had the normal tale of woe for civil servants. 'Money is very tight this year. We are probably going to have to cut some programmes.'

The alarm bells went off in my head: would our programme be among the cuts? It seemed unlikely, because we were smashing all the targets we had been set, and we were delivering something the department wanted. As casually as possible, I asked how they would decide which programmes to cut. 'Well, of course,' she said, 'we will cut the programmes that are easy to cut: low hanging fruit,' and with that she made a speedy exit.

Now the alarm bells were ringing louder than ever. She did not say that she would cut bad programmes, or underperforming ones, or big ones that would save most money. They would cut where it is easy to cut. That meant cutting programmes which were not well known, did not have high visibility and had no powerful sponsors: no one would care if they were cut. That meant our programme was in the centre of the bullseye for being cut.

Rationally, our programme should not have been targeted. But the real motivation of the department was not to do a good job; the real motivation was not to embarrass the minister by having people object to necessary cost savings. The civil servants had the same motivation as teams in any business: don't embarrass the boss, don't give the boss bad medicine.

Don't give the boss bad medicine

Over the next six months we invested heavily in making sure our programme had a very high profile, and we got the minister associated with it in public. We went from being easy to cut to being impossible to cut. If we had worked rationally, the programme would have died. By understanding the real motivation (don't embarrass the minister) we survived.

3. Build your coalition: ask for advice

If you have woven your web of influence, you have already started building your coalition of support. Now you need to convert support for you as a person into support for your project or idea. General support has to become specific and focused support. Never assume that because they support you, they will support your idea. We have already seen that users, influencers, authorisers and technical buyers all have specific interests which they have to protect and promote. You need to understand and respect their needs, not just promote your needs.

Your challenge is to convert personal goodwill into concrete support for your idea.

As an experiment, which colleague will you respond to best:

- Colleague A comes to you, tries to sell you an idea that they love, but needs your support.
- Colleague B comes to you and asks for your advice on an idea they are developing.

Most people pick colleague B because it is flattering to be asked for advice and is annoying when you are being sold. If you want to sell your idea without selling, the best way to do it is to ask for advice. You may even find that your colleagues improve your idea.

A conversation asking for advice is much easier than a conversation where you are trying to force your ideas on your colleagues. But make sure you ask for the right advice. If you ask your colleagues whether your idea is any good, you are giving everyone a veto over your idea. You are not asking for an evaluation of your idea, because you already know that you want to go ahead. You are asking for advice on how to make it happen.

By involving them at the earliest opportunity, you give them a sense of ownership over your idea. Even if they make just an obvious or trivial suggestion, be sure to thank them and show that their suggestion has improved your idea. Flattery works, and they will not argue against an idea which has their imprint on it.

Make it easy for yourself by starting with likely allies and supporters. These will be positive and constructive conversations. Starting with likely allies helps you:

- build your confidence by giving you a positive and constructive start;
- gain credibility: each stamp of approval from an ally strengthens your case;
- confirm your first allies and supporters and build momentum: create a bandwagon effect;
- discover insight into potential blockages and obstacles, and how to overcome them;
- gain insight into how you might improve your idea even further.

After talking with your allies, you should have enough support and credibility to start approaching other groups. The two key groups, which may well overlap, are the technical decision makers, influencers and potential objectors. The technical decision makers have requirements you must meet: they can veto your idea, but they cannot approve your idea. The top decision maker will not approve your idea unless all the technical decision makers give you a clean bill of health. Technical decision makers live in functions like finance, IT, HR, operations, health and safety and legal.

The earlier you involve these functional experts, the better. Give them a sense of ownership and agency. If you leave it until the last moment, you will not have a natural ally and you may well be in for some unpleasant surprises.

Outline the problem or opportunity in general terms to each functional expert. Describe what the desired outcome is and who it is for. This gives them the context they need, and it helps them understand why they need to respond to you. This is where big ideas beat small ideas every time. If you are reviewing the use of disposable cups in the office, that is worthwhile but you will go straight to the bottom of their to-do list. If you are working on a restructuring which involves their department, you will go straight to the top of their to-do list.

Do not ask them if they like or dislike your idea overall: don't give them a veto over your idea. Assume that the idea is going to happen and you want their advice on how to make it work from the perspective of their department alone. Ask financial questions to finance, people questions to HR and legal questions to legal. You need their functional expertise, not their general business judgement.

Involving the experts early allows you to explore red lines and no-go areas. They should be able to suggest broad approaches which will work. If they raise serious objections and concerns, you still have plenty of time to find solutions. You will face a challenge, not a crisis.

> **Involving the experts early allows you to explore red lines and no-go areas**

4. Deal with objections

Objections are good news. Don't run away from them and don't fight them: lean into them and make the most of them. Objections do not need to be a cause for conflict. Handle them well and they improve collaboration and improve your idea. Objections are good news for two reasons:

> **Objections are good news**

- Objections show that people care enough about your idea to take the time and effort to oppose it. This is far better than indifference. If no one cares about your idea, you go nowhere. When people oppose your idea, that shows it is important. No one risks personal and political capital on opposing an idea unless they have to.

- Objections are a very good way of improving your idea. They will help you avoid disaster and they force you to find creative solutions.

Embracing objections and obstacles is the positive and productive way to deal with them. Follow three principles and you will not only win the argument, you will win a friend as well. These three steps are far easier emotionally than having an argument:

1 Prepare, predict and pre-empt objections and obstacles.

2 Agree with the objection, don't fight it.

3 Co-create a solution.

The golden rule of dealing with conflict is to keep disagreements private and make agreements very public. In private colleagues are willing to be flexible. In public they are more likely to take a position and then stick to it: they never want to be embarrassed

> **Keep disagreements private and make agreements very public**

by changing their minds in public. In practice a private meeting is between just two people. If there are only two of you, then you both will know who has said what about the meeting after the event. As soon as there is a third person in the room, the meeting is public: no one can be sure who has said what outside the meeting.

Where you have agreement, refer to that in public. It helps you build momentum; it gives you credibility and it makes it much harder for the colleague who agreed to reverse their position. Always use the golden rule: agree in public, disagree in private.

Following the three steps and the golden rule works 90 per cent of the time. It is an easy and collaborative way of dealing with problems. Ten per cent of the time it does not work. This is where you need Plan B, which we explore in Chapter 6.

Prepare, predict and pre-empt objections

Part of the art of management is to develop a highly tuned risk radar. You should know how all your colleagues operate: some are open and honest, some may be more grumpy and negative. They all have different sorts of expertise and expectations. Before you discuss your idea with any of your colleagues, you should be able to predict how they are likely to react. To help you predict, take advice from other colleagues on where they see the potential obstacles and who might raise objections. Use your risk radar to give you an early warning of problems ahead. You should never be surprised by an objection. If you are surprised, it is much harder to deal with it. If you know the objection is coming, you can prepare for it and pre-empt it.

> **You should never be surprised by an objection**

Pre-empting objections is a powerful way of dealing with them. If you know that a colleague will raise an objection, don't let them raise it. Raise it yourself for them. This changes the terms of the debate. You are no longer having to argue about their idea or objection, which is an impossible task because they will be emotionally attached to the very clever problem they have spotted. Instead, you are inviting them to use their expertise to help you solve a problem you have identified. Ask for their help in finding a solution. Even if you think you know the solution, ask them for their solution. They will own their solution and be committed to helping you implement it.

You can pre-empt objections simply. For instance, if you are speaking to HR and you know they will be concerned about how staff will react to your proposed changes. Raise this concern with them and ask them how staff reactions can best be managed. You change HR from being adversaries that create obstacles for you to overcome into being allies that help you overcome obstacles.

Agree with the objection, don't fight it

When someone disagrees with you, it can feel like they are not just attacking your idea, they are attacking you. This leads to an emotional and defensive response which is the start of a slippery slope: you and your colleague will become ever more entrenched in your views and no amount of logic or reason will resolve it. Even if you think you have won the argument, you will have lost an ally.

The first step is not to react emotionally: don't be negative or defensive. The difference between a good reaction and a poor reaction is precisely three seconds. That is how long you should take before replying, so that you can gather your thoughts. A good way of buying time is to ask, 'Say more?' or something similar. Let the other person explain their thoughts while you consider your response.

An even better way of reacting is to paraphrase the objection back to your colleague. Paraphrasing is the art of summarising what the other person said, but in your own words. This helps because it:

- buys you time to think about your full response;
- respects your colleague because it shows that they have been heard and understood;
- clarifies and confirms the issue: if there is misunderstanding, your paraphrasing will highlight that immediately.

Once you have agreed and clarified the issue, you can proceed to the third step: ask for their solution.

Co-create a solution

A favourite, and destructive, sport that some people play in meetings is the objections game. Finding a problem is an easy way to show that you are smart, and then you have the joy of sitting back and watching others squirm as they try to find a solution. It is a game which teaches everyone that it is not worth having ideas in meetings because you are likely to be shot down by someone trying to prove how clever they are. Do not let colleagues play this game, because you cannot win.

If you have agreed that there is an obstacle or objection to be dealt with, ask them how they would deal with it. This judo throw turns the tables on them. They now have to prove that they are smart enough to identify solutions, not just problems.

Most colleagues will make an effort. They will offer some half-formed ideas. However good or bad the idea may be, run with it.

Show respect for your colleague by building on their idea. You can now start a productive process of co-creating a solution.

Occasionally, colleagues will be unhelpful. They will deflect the problem back to you, or they will offer such outrageously implausible conditions for solving the problem that you will know that they do not want to help you. Usually, this is a sign that the problem is not entirely rational. The rational objection is likely to be a smokescreen for an emotional or political objection. There is no point fighting an emotional problem with logic: it will not work.

Enjoy the $1 billion obstacle course

For slightly obscure reasons, I decided to start a bank. After some initial research I discovered that this would require at least $1 billion in capital. I checked my bank account and I was at least $1 billion short of the required capital. Even worse, I had experienced serious difficulty in getting my credit card limit raised by $1,000: I was forever trying to navigate unhelpful algorithms or navigate unhelpful and disempowered call centre staff.

Inadvertently, I followed the five-step process outlined in this chapter.

I started with the big idea of the bank (Step 1) and then discussed it with confidantes and allies I could trust (Step 2). They massively improved the idea which changed from being an internet retail bank to being an internet commercial bank focused on SMEs with a turnover of $10 million to $100 million a year. Not only did they help with the radical change, they also helped identify other potential allies and investors and made introductions to me. That allowed me to move to Step 3: socialising the idea with key players. Each key player I talked to added to the credibility of the proposal and to the momentum of the project.

Step 3 rapidly moved to Step 4: endless objections started to appear. These were massively helpful for two reasons. First,

---

each objection was a chance to strengthen and improve the business plan. Second, because it was a big idea, I found myself talking to the right people. I did not have to deal with unhelpful algorithms or unhelpful call centre staff. I was dealing with executive-level decision makers.

These objections took me all the way to the CEO of a bank. The objections had empowered me and given me confidence. I had heard and resolved every possible objection. All I had to do was to move to Step 5: confirm the agreement in private, and then in public.

The CEO asked me how much the plan would cost. 'About a billion,' I replied as casually as I could.

'Good,' he said, 'if you had asked for anything less you would not have been credible.' It turns out that asking a bank for $1 billion is easier than asking it for $1,000. A big idea beats a small idea every time. Be bold and recognise objections as your friends, not foes.

5. Confirm agreement in private, then in public

This is the most important, and easiest, step of the process. By now, you will have done all the hard work. You will have built your coalition of support, you will have identified all the potential obstacles and dealt with them. You will have done this largely in private, in one-to-one meetings with key stakeholders. Individually they support you, but they need the reassurance that they are not alone in supporting you.

You now need to convert that private and individual support into public and collective support. Public support cements your position, and leaves any potential doubters very isolated. Most of them will decide that it is not worth having a public battle which they will lose: their opposition will quietly melt away.

The most obvious way to confirm the collective decision is to hold a meeting with all the key stakeholders. As ever, do not use the meeting to make a decision: use the meeting to confirm the consensus you have achieved in private.

A meeting can be too time consuming for a wide group of stakeholders, in which case you can craft an email or newsletter which either comes from you, or from the project sponsor or from the CEO.

Summary

If you master the art of selling without selling, you can start to achieve great impact. But the greater your desired impact, the more opposition you will face. You will find that standard selling techniques are not enough. You need to find ways of overcoming the opposition that any big idea will inevitably face. You can discover how to do this in the next chapter.

chapter 6

Overcoming obstacles: politics and the art of the hustle

The bigger the decision, the greater the opposition. Fighting opposition is painful and rarely works: even if you win the argument, you lose an ally. You

The bigger the decision, the greater the opposition

have to find ways of winning without fighting. Welcome to the art of the hustle.

The challenge of the corporate obstacle course

If you are going to make a difference, you are going to upset someone. You will possibly upset a lot of people, if they feel threatened by your changes. This means you should welcome opposition: it shows that you will make an impact and that you are being taken seriously.

The good news is that it is far easier to deal with opposition than it is to deal with indifference. Where there is opposition, there is energy and momentum which you can shift in your direction with the right approach. Where there is indifference, no one cares about your idea. That is a sign that you are working on the wrong agenda, or an agenda of no importance.

Chapter 5 focused on selling when the wind is more or less behind you: you can make steady progress towards your target provided you do not make any big mistakes. Most of the time that sort of selling works, especially where you are dealing with routine matters. If your project is part of an agreed plan, or part of a predictable annual cycle, then standard selling techniques work.

This chapter is for those occasions when you are attempting something non-routine, which has bigger potential impact and you find yourself encountering strong opposition. The selling techniques in Chapter 5 still apply, but you need to raise your game significantly to deal with the much more challenging world you now encounter.

The best managers are like the best trades and craft people: they are defined by their ability to deal with the unexpected, the complicated and the unusual. These are the moments when the instruction manual is no use. Average tradespeople and managers can cope with the routine when you can follow the rules, follow procedures, follow the manual. The best managers thrive when the rules, procedures and manuals no longer help. This is when you need a combination of deep skill, creativity, experience and commitment. In practice this comes down to two things: you need both the right mindset and the right skill set.

This chapter shows how you can acquire both the right mindset and skill set to overcome obstacles.

Overcoming obstacles: mindset and the art of the hustle

The secret to overcoming obstacles is the same as the secret of productivity: own your idea, own your project, own your work. Act like an owner, not like a disempowered body for hire. You have

Act like an owner, not like a disempowered body for hire

probably already experienced this, or seen colleagues act like this. When you own an idea which really matters to you, immediately you will start displaying all the behaviours which will lead to success:

- Spot opportunities and act on them.
- Find the courage to step up when others step back.
- Overcome obstacles and resistance to your ideas.
- Force yourself out of your comfort zone to try new things, introduce yourself to important people, have difficult conversations.
- Take the initiative: make the agenda, not take the agenda.
- Display confidence, conviction and belief in your idea.
- Forge alliances with people not like yourself by finding out what motivates them.
- Work outside your area of responsibility.
- Keep pushing ahead while others step aside or drop out.
- Negotiate resources, support and influence beyond your formal job title.
- Discover your creative self in solving problems and dealing with people.
- Never take 'no' for an answer: discover that 'no' is simply a prelude to 'yes'.
- Fail to understand the word 'impossible'.

All these behaviours are the product of the ownership mindset. This mindset comes from deep commitment to your idea and belief in your idea. When you believe in your idea, you believe in yourself. You do not need to develop self-confidence, passion or enthusiasm; you do not need to go an assertiveness course. All these things come naturally when you are committed to an idea you believe in.

These behaviours are a consistent pattern among high-impact managers, including all of those featured in this book. Although the behaviours are consistent and successful, the management literature has no name for them, although we all recognise this sort of behaviour: it is called hustle.

Hustle is highly divisive, and is a very good way of sorting out high-impact managers from the rest. Many managers recoil at the idea of hustle. They do not want to be seen like a property developer always looking for the next deal and always teetering on the edge of morality and legality. If that is how you think of hustle, you are probably right to try and avoid it.

But hustle is not like that. High-impact managers nearly always recognise the importance of hustle, in any culture.

Hustle in any culture

Amir is a senior professional based in Kuala Lumpur, working for a multinational manufacturing firm. Malaysia is typically regarded as a high respect culture where you do not give bad medicine to the boss, and you do not hustle. Amir challenges both those assumptions. First, he points out that even within the Malaysian operations there are many different cultures: marketing in Kuala Lumpur will be very different from operations in the factories. But even so, hustle in Malaysia??

Amir describes not only the need to hustle, but how to do it in a culturally appropriate way:

'Of course you have to hustle. But you have to display respect although that is not submission. This is very delicate. It is about the tone of voice and the words used. How it does not work is when you are pushy, brash or lacking respect. It is always

---

best to link your request to an idea or the priority of the boss. That is the safest way. You have to link your ask to something that is top of mind for the boss. You have to contextualise your conversation.'

Although hustle matters wherever you are, it is easier in cultures with low power distance than high power distance (more democratic than deferential cultures). Noemi Hernandez describes the expectations of a female manager in Latin America:

You are just expected to work, work, work and wait to get noticed. We are just grateful to have a job so it is very complicated to ask for more money or ask for promotion. And as a woman it is even more complicated because you are meant to be quiet in a machismo culture.

But she realised that would get her nowhere: 'I had to challenge my own beliefs and personality. I find the American style of me, me, me very difficult. So I make it about my work and not just about myself. That is how I have to sell myself.' Many people are like Noemi: they do not like self-promotion. Instead, focus on promoting your mission and your work. Your hustle does not have to be about 'me, me, me', it can be about 'we, we, we'. That sort of hustle is appreciated anywhere.

Hustle is often best when it is, as Amir suggests, subtle and discreet. That smartly dressed executive in front of you may look too suave to hustle. Don't be fooled. If she is someone who really makes things happen, she has probably learned the art of the hustle, and knows how to use it in influential places.

Hustle comes naturally to people under two circumstances: a personal crisis or they find a compelling mission. Having a major personal crisis is not ideal as a career management tool: you will do better by finding an idea which you want to own, grow and develop.

Anyone who has achieved anything of note has had to overcome opposition and adversity and make things happen with minimal resources. The examples in this book would have been impossible without the hustle mindset:

- gaining the support of Saudi, Qatari and Omani governments for an expedition across the Empty Quarter of Saudi Arabia;
- starting Teach First, which became the largest graduate recruiter in the UK;
- starting Tapoly, or Unlocked, (see later in the chapter): all entrepreneurs learn the art of the hustle;
- taking on UNGA and making it a successful event.

Hustle is the magic which enables you to create something out of nothing. Having no role, no power, no budget and no resources should not be an obstacle to making an impact. For instance, Kate Adams worked in the civil service. That is a context which is associated more with structure, reliability and order than with the world of hustle and adversity. In the course of her work, she met some former child soldiers and was appalled by their stories. She decided that something had to be done, and she would do it. So how do you tackle any of the problems of children in conflict when you have no power, no budget, no support? Here is how Kate hustled to make it happen:

> **Hustle is the magic which enables you to create something out of nothing**

> **Having no role, no power, no budget and no resources should not be an obstacle to making an impact**

- She wrangled leave from her government department to work as an intern at War Child where she had no formal role.
- She discovered War Child had no policy or advocacy department, so set one up for them.
- She saw a policy director at the Foreign Office do a speech on war and women victims of sexual violence. Kate cornered him after the speech and suggested that if he did not include children and men as victims of sexual violence, then that could cause embarrassment to the minister. He would be criticised for not being inclusive. No civil servant wants to embarrass the minister.

- She got seconded to the Foreign Office to prepare a summit meeting on sexual violence with the foreign secretary and Angelina Jolie. Once again, had no role, no budget, no contacts, no agenda.

Kate takes up the story in which she hustles to make the Angelina Jolie event a success with no budget or role: 'My role was unclear so on the first day I had to come up with ideas and define my role. I had zero budget. I had to go deep into my black book to find people who would be able to help. I got rejected many times, for instance by the Tate Gallery. But then I found another gallery with a massive sculpture which they agreed to install for free. All they wanted in return was a picture of the sculpture and artist with Angelina Jolie. This lack of budget makes you very resourceful. I also made a silent cinema which involved people wearing headphones costing £200 each. I went out to civil society to get the material to show the silent cinema. I realised it was easy to get free resource when you tell people that we have a room full of ministers.'

From having nothing and being in the wrong place, Kate found a way of producing a summit which dealt with the difficult subject of sexual violence against men and boys in war. Necessity is the mother of invention. When your back is against the wall, when there is something you deeply believe in, you will find a way through. You will learn to hustle without being taught to hustle.

The best way to learn hustle is to take on a project which has real meaning to you and excites you. You do not need to take wild risks. Just start pushing yourself beyond your comfort zone, little by little, as you take on ever more exciting and audacious assignments.

Start pushing yourself beyond your comfort zone

Some of the most exceptional leaders I interview have had both a major life crisis and a meaningful life mission. As philosopher Nietzsche (nearly) wrote: that which does not break you, makes you stronger. Adversity turns out to be a great call to action. For instance:

- homeless with an addiction as a teenager, now the founder and CEO of Unlocked, which recruits graduates to be outstanding prison officers;

- given one month to live and a 1 per cent chance of survival as a teenager; now a senior *gaijin* (foreign) executive at Hitachi and a member of the old Emperor's tennis club;
- failed at A Levels and at university, now general counsel at Salesforce.

Being grateful for adversity

Janthana Kaenprakhamroy is the co-CEO and founder of Tapoly, the award-winning insurtech.

'When I was eight years old, my father left, leaving me to care for my much younger brother. Soon after, my mother moved to Sweden. This meant I was responsible for putting food on the table and covering all expenses, including school fees. To make ends meet, I took on labour jobs, and my school provided a grant. Growing up in a village in northeast Thailand, I would forage in the forest for fruit or fish from the rice farm to feed us. At the time, I didn't feel sorry for myself – I thought everyone was as poor as we were. But looking back, if I saw an eight year old in the same situation, I would definitely cry. My family didn't offer much help, and the village was so poor that it made people focus only on themselves.

Thanks to one of my mother's cousins who was already in Sweden, my mother was able to move there to help her cousin after she had her second child. This eventually allowed my mother to find paid work. Through her cousin's introduction, my mother met a kind Swedish man who welcomed us into his family. This opened the door for me to join my mother in Sweden, where I finally had the opportunity to get an education.

As a founder, resilience is crucial. From a very young age, I learned how to solve problems on my own and take responsibility for my family. Many founders who haven't experienced much hardship growing up and are faced with

---

> huge responsibilities may struggle when challenges arise, sometimes even giving up, because they lack the grit to overcome adversity. I, on the other hand, am grateful for my challenges – they taught me how to endure and thrive.'

These are people who have all looked deep into the abyss. Having found their way out of oblivion, they have re-engaged with life with double the vigour and commitment. They have no intention of wasting their lives.

As a career move, it is probably unwise to become addicted or homeless, fail at school, have a mental breakdown, become bankrupt or go through a near-death experience. But we can learn from such people. Life is very precious and we only get one shot at it. Choose how you want to make the most of it. A good choice is to focus on family and friends and have a good work–life balance. Another choice is to find meaning, mission and pride in your work.

> **Life is very precious and we only get one shot at it**

Overcoming obstacles: beyond reason

Economists like to pretend that humans are rational. Psychotherapists would disagree. Management lives in the grey space between the rational world of economists and the emotional world of psychotherapists, with one additional twist: all organisations are deeply political. This means that when you encounter obstacles, you have to recognise that they are:

- rational;
- emotional;
- political.

We are taught from school onwards to deal with rational problems rationally. There is always a model answer which you can put down on paper. The world of work is different. The rational case clearly matters: if you have no rational case, then you have no case at all. But when you face opposition, the rational case is at best relatively unimportant. Often, it is positively harmful to you. Nobody likes to be outsmarted and nobody likes to be proven wrong or made to look stupid in public. If you are very smart and pummel your opposition with your intellectual brilliance you may well win the argument, but you will also make enemies who will find ways of returning your disfavour.

Nobody likes to be outsmarted

For instance, Kenji Okada who became CFO of Tokio Marine Holdings ruefully looked back on his early career: 'I was very high IQ, but not so high EQ. I was famous for my IQ. So I had many battles as a result of low EQ. Reputation really matters in a membership organisation.' (Japanese firms with lifetime employment are often referred to as membership organisations.) Fortunately, he was smart enough to work out that being smart is not enough. In the case below, he shows how he combined rational, emotional and political nous to make a major change.

Rational, emotional and political hustle

Kenji Okada of Tokio Marine Holdings was appointed as head of internal audit. Internal audit was not effective enough because it was very fragmented. He wanted to strengthen it and give it more authority. That meant taking the function away from each subsidiary and centralising it. He did not have the authority to do this.

He describes how he went about it. Note how he combines rational, emotional and political hustle very discreetly, methodically and effectively by building consensus at all levels.

'When I arrived in internal audit, staff had no blueprint for the future. So the first thing I did was to benchmark global best practices among the leading insurers to see how they managed internal audit *(Rational)*. I then shared my blueprint with my staff. I spoke with each team around the world and asked, "do you want to report locally or do you want to report to a global internal audit function?" The majority of them said that they wanted to report to the global function because they could see the benefits of it to them and for their authority *(Emotional and Political)*.

I then went to every president of the small to medium-sized domestic companies and had one-to-one meetings with them to show how these changes would be beneficial to them. I would centralise the service and as a result would be able to provide a better service to each of them *(Rational, Emotional and Political)*. Nearly everyone agreed. But in one case I gave up trying to integrate internal audit because he did not want to. So they are staying as they were. But I have not given up yet. I will be patient. Things will change and then I will be able to integrate that function *(Political)*.'

Doing this showed that he could execute well: he was promoted to chief risk officer and is now CFO.

Contrast Okada's approach with the more rational approach taken by Paul Bennett when he was in leadership and development at Lloyds Banking Group.

Being right is never enough

'We aimed to introduce a new tool for use across Lloyds, feeling confident in its inherent value and proven benefits. We believed this would be enough to secure approval, but we soon realised this assumption was wrong and that there were additional factors to consider. We didn't fully account for the broader network of stakeholders and influencers. Having presumed that it was an obvious decision, we soon encountered unexpected concerns. Some felt the tool was too complex, preferring the

➤

simplicity of the existing solution with which they were already familiar.

While we were excited about the new tool, we overlooked the importance of focusing on users' needs and experiences, a classic marketing dilemma. It was a valuable lesson in understanding that even a great product requires alignment with the lived experiences of the users. We learned the importance of communicating the problem, demonstrating why change is needed, and then getting out and telling a compelling story that connects an old problem with a new solution, and articulating the "why"; why the ways we had tried before fell short of what we could now achieve, and how much better things could be with the proposed solution.'

Repeatedly, I hear executives complain that their brilliant case which is absolutely bulletproof fails. They get very frustrated. The problem is not about the words and the numbers: it is about the people and the politics. Even with the best case in the world, you still have to work the people and the politics. This is especially important when you run into opposition.

Opposition to an idea or an initiative is always expressed in rational terms. In a meeting, how often do you hear rational objections such as, 'it is too expensive, the customers won't like it, it will cannibalise our existing sales, it is too risky.'

How often do you hear emotional and political objections such as, 'it will take power from me, threaten my status, take resources from my initiative, make life complicated for me, cause me more work, make it harder for me to meet my year end targets.'

Rational objections are easy to deal with. But usually, they are cover for emotional and political objections. This creates a huge bear trap. The unwary manager will hear the rational objection and lead a rational onslaught of data and research to prove their point. This leads to an increasingly acrimonious argument which goes nowhere because the real issue is not being dealt with. Like

Okada, you have to be smart enough to know that it is not enough to be smart. If you want to overcome opposition, you have to deal with the people and the politics first. If you do that, the rational argument becomes a formality. The challenge, as ever, is knowing how to deal with the people and the politics. That is the focus of the rest of this section.

> **You have to be smart enough to know that it is not enough to be smart**

Overcoming obstacles: the art and skill of politics

I ran into a brick wall once. After leaving hospital with several stitches in my head, I realised that if you are confronted with a brick wall, it is smarter to run around it, even if it takes a little bit more time. I had discovered, the painful way, the key to hustling your way past opposition. If you run straight at the opposition, you will get a very sore head. You have to find a way around the opposition. Before dealing with the opposition, find your allies and find your leverage points. If you have enough allies and leverage, the opposition will melt away because they will be the ones looking at attacking the brick wall of all your allies and support.

When faced with opposition, naïve managers attack the opposition head on. This is always ugly, and success is not guaranteed. Even if you succeed, it comes at the price of losing friends and influence. More politically astute managers do not focus on attacking the opposition: they focus on building support and leverage.

The simplest way to find enough leverage and allies is to be acting on the instructions of the CEO or another power figure. If you have the support of the CEO, use it wisely and use it sparingly. The CEO is probably happy to support you and your agenda, and to celebrate your successes: they will be much less happy if you use their authority to make people do things. One of the few occasions I have seen CEOs become visibly frustrated is when a staff member pushed her agenda by claiming she was acting on the wishes of the CEO. Claiming the support of the CEO for your agenda is dangerous. At best, it shows you are weak because you cannot make the case yourself; at worst, you undermine your CEO by doing something without their knowledge or support.

How to use the backing of your CEO

Sri Chandana Nagoji is head of philanthropy at Salesforce India. Both the CEO and COO support her and her work, but Sri Chandana does not use that support to direct or coerce colleagues into doing things. Here is how she uses it, in her words:

'Both the CEO and COO have been very proactive in giving back. So they have been our champions. It helps that the top two leaders in India have my back. The CEO says I should be asking her for more support so that she can help promote me. But she is very busy. So I am cautious about asking her for too much. But she can put in kind words for me. The CEO will tweet in support of our success. Even a simple tweet is a strong demonstration of support for what we are doing. That obviously helps in dealing with other leaders in the organisation.'

Sri Chandana uses CEO support the right way. She uses it indirectly to build influence, rather than directly to enforce decisions.

More often, you have to overcome opposition without the direct or indirect support of a CEO. This is where you have to be creative and find your allies and find your points of leverage in the system. There will always be plenty of people who say 'no' and want to stop you. You cannot fight them all, so don't fight them. Instead, find the people who say 'yes': start building momentum with them.

Here are the five key principles for dealing with opposition:

1 Don't fight the opposition head on, unless there is no alternative.

2 Make the rational case for change, but don't rely on it.

3 Find your allies and what motivates them. Use your first allies to find more allies.

4 Find your points of leverage: control of budget, customers, information, expertise, ideas, etc.

5 Move to action: create momentum and change the reality on the ground.

If you follow these principles, the opposition melts away: they do not want to argue against the brick wall of allies you have assembled, and they do not want to argue with the reality you have created on the ground.

The principles are easy to express, hard to execute. In practice, it will not be clear who your allies are or what motivates them; your opposition is likely to shapeshift and be hard to pin down; your points of leverage may be weak and building momentum is never easy. This is where you need to hustle: you need to keep trying new things, approaching different people, seeking advice and spotting opportunities when they arise.

The first principle of avoiding conflict surprises naïve managers who believe that obstacles and objections must lead to conflict. This belief leads to two poor outcomes. The first poor outcome is a pitched battle: regardless of who wins, you create enemies and there is blood on the floor. The second poor outcome is that the naïve manager retreats or surrenders, which leads to the end of the idea. More astute managers understand that the best way to win is without fighting. In this, they echo Chinese philosopher Sun Tzu, who wrote *The Art of War* roughly 2,500 years ago. He laid out three conditions for fighting a war, which apply as much for today's corporate warriors as they did for Chinese warriors 2,500 years ago. His three conditions are:

• Only fight when there is a prize worth fighting for.

• Only fight when there is no other way of achieving your goal.

• Only fight when you know you will win.

Most battles within organisations fail at least one, and sometimes all three, of these tests. If your idea is big enough, it will pass the first test: it is worth fighting for. That leaves the second two tests. In practice, you can usually win without fighting.

The five principles above are principles, not a logical sequence of steps. In practice, you work all of the steps at the same time. The more you talk to potential allies, the better you can make your rational case and the more you can identify potential points of leverage and quick wins to build momentum. This very messy, exciting and tiring process is the art of the hustle.

Understanding and applying these principles is not the same as following a cookbook or a financial textbook. If it was that easy and predictable, then AI would be able to take over and most managers would find that they are redundant. Fortunately, dealing with objections and making change happen is far beyond the capability of AI.

The way to learn these principles is through experience. This can be a slow and painful way to learn. We need a way of learning from experience at speed. Business schools know exactly how to do this: they use the case method of discovery: learn from the relevant experience of people who have faced this challenge before. So in the finest tradition of Harvard, INSEAD and Stanford business schools, here are three cases which illustrate how you can apply the principles of hustle and politics to overcome obstacles and make an impact.

The two cases below highlight different principles and show how you have to be flexible and creative in applying the principles. Every situation is both unique and volatile, which requires a unique and flexible solution. One size does not fit all.

In the first case, Walter Emberger faced overwhelming opposition to his idea of recruiting great graduates to teach in schools in disadvantaged areas in Austria. He was not a politician, had no education experience and had no resources and the whole system was against him. Although he could make the rational case, emotionally everyone felt very threatened by this challenge to how they did things, and politically he had no support. His idea was dead in the water.

With no power, expertise, support or resources how do you change a system which does not want to be changed? Although Walter followed all five principles, the big difference was that he changed the reality on the ground.

You can argue against an idea; it is much harder to argue against reality

Instead of arguing about the idea, he found an ally who would let him test the idea in one area. You can argue against an idea; it is much harder to argue against reality.

Changing a system which does not want to be changed: Teach for Austria

Here is how Walter saw the challenge: 'I thought the idea was so beautiful that it would be obvious. But the education system did not want us and did not believe that anyone could teach without the full traditional training. Teach for Austria meant that their way of doing things was threatened and the whole system felt threatened, so they did not want it. And of course, we could not prove it until we had done it, but we could not do it until we had proven it.

At the end of a meeting one of the officials stood up and said that the education system is fine as it is and we do not need to change anything. He then asked: "Do you have any political support for your idea?" I had never thought about that.'

Here is how Walter addressed the challenge, using the five principles outlined above:

- *Make the rational case,* which gave Walter the ammunition required to fix meetings where he discovered who supported his idea and who opposed it (virtually everyone).

- *Find allies*: as a resident of Salzburg, Walter eventually got a meeting with the governor who backed his idea. She was powerful within the governing SDP and wanted to make a difference. Walter had found his opening.

➤

- *Find your point of leverage*: Walter discovered that he did not need national approval for his idea.
- *Make the emotional case*. Reports can be argued about; it is harder to argue with reality. Walter arranged for the governor of Salzburg to visit Teach First in England, which was already successful and prestigious.
- *Change the reality on the ground*. Walter started in Salzburg and Vienna, much to the fury of ministry officials in Vienna who had not given him permission. He called Teach for Austria a 'special project' which did not need permission, so he just kept going. The officials did not have the power to stop him.
- *Use allies to find more allies*. Walter arranged for the governor of Salzburg to introduce him to the mayor of Vienna. By then, she was effectively his sponsor so she did more than introduce him. She had briefed the mayor and his officials, so they were all supportive. Teach for Austria went ahead in Vienna and Salzburg without federal approval.

Watch the opposition melt away. Eventually, a new education minister was appointed and approval was granted, although never in writing: reality on the ground was recognised.

In the second case, the stakes were very high: lives were being lost because humanitarian aid was being blocked because of conflict. How can you unblock the aid and save lives when you have no political power? This case turns on finding some unlikely leverage against a very powerful blocker, and then building an alliance to use that leverage.

Using political acupuncture to save lives

Nicola Reindorp is CEO of pioneering organisation Crisis Action which has a unique coalition-building model to catalyse action to protect civilians from conflict. In 2013, Crisis Action and the humanitarian and human rights groups it helps were faced with a huge challenge: how to get humanitarian aid into Syria. At the time, Syria was in a civil war, the economy was collapsing and the government was stopping any aid getting to where it was most needed: rebel-held areas. As aid agencies battled with Syrian government red tape and the humanitarian need among the population increased, one proposal emerged: convince the UN Security Council to authorise aid convoys to cross from Syria's neighbouring countries directly into Syria's rebel-held areas without waiting for Syrian President Assad's assent. The problem: Russia supported the Syrian government, in part to sustain its vital port access to the Mediterranean. Russia also had a veto on the UN Security Council, so could block any motion the Syrian government disliked. So how to get UN Security Council approval for aid to go where it was needed?

Here is how Crisis Action went about it:

Identify key supporters. Key supporters on the Security Council included the United States, UK and France. But in the face of possible veto from Russia or China, their support risked entrenching Russian opposition. Crisis Action needed to find supporters who would bring neutral countries on board with the measure, isolating Russia and perhaps persuading it not to veto the measure. A first key step was ensuring the Security Council heard a clear message from the UN's leading humanitarian official, a position then held by Baroness Valerie Amos, a former government official from the UK. Crisis Action coordinated a letter from 15 aid agencies to write to ask her to demand action from the Security Council to get aid to those in need and save lives. Crisis Action then arranged for doctors in Syria to draft a letter explaining the horrendous situation: that was published in the Lancet with support from doctors around the world. Because doctors are seen to be neutral, that generated momentum.

Identify the key leverage points. Another key moment in the campaign came as Russia was preparing to host the winter Olympics in Sochi: it was a chance to gain global prestige. Putin did not want it spoiled by negative media coverage. This gave Crisis Action leverage. This time, working with another ally, former US Secretary of State Madeleine Albright and some of her former foreign minister peers, Crisis Action was able to secure a letter of support for a proposed UN resolution signed by 51 eminent individuals, including former heads of state, appealing to President Putin to 'give the world an Olympic opening' and concede to a Security Council resolution authorising aid trucks to cross Syria's borders even in the face of the Syrian government's blockade. On the day of the vote at the UN, all the delegates found a copy of the *New York Times* in front of them, with a large advertisement making the case for support: that was paid for by a donor. The leverage points were used to squeeze Russia both in public and in private.

Identify the blockers. Crisis Action identified two blockers. Russia was the obvious blocker, but was vulnerable because of Putin's concern for his image on the eve of Sochi. The second blocker was legal: member states were nervous about the legality of interfering in the internal affairs of another member state. Crisis Action persuaded the ex-head of the UN's Office of Legal Affairs to be among a coalition of lawyers writing a joint letter showing that the resolution would be legal.

As a result, resolutions 2139 and then 2165 were passed by the UN and aid convoys were allowed into Syria from neighbouring countries, avoiding Syrian government control. Many lives were saved. Reflecting on the experience, Nicola said: 'We think of our campaigning as acupuncture. Find the point in the body that will relieve the pressure. It is not about sitting in a warm bath and hoping the pain goes. You need very precise pressure and often you need a series of acupuncture points to succeed.'

The final case once again involves building a coalition, based on understanding where the leverage really lies. In this case, power is largely about influence rather than position or budget. The result is that the leverage points and essential allies are not in the obvious places. You have to be creative when finding leverage points and building alliances, as this case illustrates.

Navigating a global decision

The Commonwealth is an IGO (intergovernmental organisation) with 56 member states. Steve Cutts was asked to lead an effort to refocus resources more efficiently: this is an intensely political exercise because there is always the risk of creating winners and losers. The head of the Commonwealth could not simply mandate the shift, because power is vested with the member states.

Steve had to work out where the decision-making power really lay, and how to build a coalition in support of change. His first insight was that for 'most decisions in IGOs the member state governments do not care' because the budget is too small. Instead, 'they give authority to their heads of delegation, but the heads of delegation don't care about management either'. Decision making was not at the top. Real power lay in the middle: these are the shadowy 'sherpas' who quietly work in the background before and after every big summit meeting between nations.

Identifying the sherpas was just the first step. The second step was to build the coalition of support: it would be impossible to convince all 56 nations individually, because there are not enough hours in the day. He had to find the right pressure points and right influencers within the system. He makes it sound simple: 'I started with the UK, New Zealand, Canada and Australia because they are the people who pay the money and fund the organisation. You also need to know who the influencers are in each region. For instance, my head of office came from Sierra Leone and could talk to African member states very well. I also realised that the Antigua and Barbuda high commissioner was very influential with the Caribbean member states so I made sure that I got him on board early.' With this critical mass of money, power and opinion in support, Steve was able to get the much needed financial reforms accepted.

Cases, like the past, can be very deceptive. When history is written it can all look logical and inevitable. But in the present, nothing seems logical or inevitable. There is a cascade of unpredictable events and people, and you can feel like you are fighting fog. The purpose of the cases above is to show that even in the chaos of the present, there are principles you can follow to find your way past the most entrenched opposition.

You have to be creative. For instance, William Wan is the general secretary of the Kindness Movement in Singapore, which was part of the civil service. William was clear that you cannot have a kindness movement where the government and civil service are telling people to be kind: it has to be a people's movement. But how do you persuade the government and civil service to set you free and lose control? Politically it was a non-starter. But William realised he had some unlikely leverage: his age. He was above the retirement age for civil servants, so they had no hold over him. He could speak out if he wanted. No civil servant wants an unnecessary public battle which could embarrass the minister. So he gained independence and proceeded to have campaign successes such as improving the return rate of trays at food hawker centres from 35 per cent (not very kind or considerate) to 88 per cent (much kinder). William realised his age meant that the government could not push him around: he had a very unlikely source of leverage. You always have leverage, if you look for it.

> **You always have leverage, if you look for it**

If you find it hard and you face deep opposition, that probably means you are doing something worthwhile. If it was easy, someone would have done it already. If there is no opposition, you are probably not making a real difference.

> **Deep opposition probably means you are doing something worthwhile**

When things get tough, stay optimistic and believe in your mission. If you are not optimistic and do not believe in your mission, no one else will be optimistic for you or believe in the mission either.

Optimism is not about hoping to get lucky, because luck is not a method and hope is not a strategy. Optimism is never doubting that you will prevail and doing what it takes to succeed. Follow the principles above, keep hustling and savour success when you finally achieve it.

Summary

By now, you have all the tools you need to amplify your formal power and make things happen beyond your area of responsibility. But if you want to make even more impact, you will need to increase your formal power as well as your informal power. Discover how to do this in the next chapter.

---

chapter 7

Read the air: growing your formal power

Management involves acquiring and exercising power.
The more power you have, the more impact you can have.
Acquiring more formal power enables you to have more
impact: promotion helps you do more and achieve more. This
chapter shows how formal and informal power grow together
and how you can acquire more formal power.

The challenge of promotion, power and impact

It is easier for the CEO to have an impact than for the janitor. Formal power still matters. Despite the rhetoric of flat organisations, there is still a hierarchy. If you are at the top, you have more budget, resources and decision-making rights than people at the bottom.

If you want to make an impact, formal power helps you. Formal power amplifies your informal power and informal power amplifies your formal power. They reinforce each other. Use them well and they pull each other up; use them poorly and they pull each other down.

> **Informal power amplifies your formal power**

The obvious conclusion is that if you want to make a bigger impact, you should seek promotion. Most firms are set up to encourage competition for promotion. This was explicit at a large Japanese insurer which greeted 100 new graduate recruits with a simple message: 'Welcome to the tournament'. The tournament was scheduled to last 40 years: the length of their career. Roughly one in eight would succeed; others would be gently moved aside into less demanding roles or into the less secure world of a subsidiary company.

The goals and the rules of the tournament differ by country. In the United States, few people expect that the tournament will be played out in just one firm. Average job tenure is under three years for the 25–34-year-old age group, which rises to ten years for the 55- to 64-year-old cohort. 'Career' is both a verb and a noun: in Japan it is a noun which is shorthand for the one-firm tournament. In the United States 'career' is a verb which describes how people career from one firm to another, and from triumph to disaster and back again.

> **'Career' is both a verb and a noun**

Career may be a verb or a noun for you, but in both cases you face the same question: 'Do I want promotion?'

The obvious answer should be, 'Yes, I want promotion'. Promotion offers the chance to make more impact and make more money, in return for more responsibility. The more surprising answer came from many outstanding individuals who are already making an impact: they really, deeply do not want promotion.

Successful people give three legitimate reasons for not wanting promotion, and they are connected:

- Professionals have a craft skill which they have carefully honed, and they want to keep on doing it. If you are great at coding, selling, teaching or data analysis it is a fair call to want to keep doing that. Such professionals recognise that promotion means a change of role: they will no longer be able to focus on their craft skill. Instead, they will have to learn management skills, which they often regard as complete BS.

- Professionals who work on the front line see the day-to-day impact they are making, and they enjoy the rush and excitement of doing that. They do not want to trade the front line for a desk job.

- If you obsess about promotion, you will get very frustrated in a flat organisation because there are not enough promotions to go around. You need to think in wider career terms:

  - Am I doing enjoyable work?
  - Do I have colleagues I want to work with?
  - Will I be able to learn and grow in this role?
  - Can I have acceptable work–life balance?

These reasons were summarised by one executive who has not been promoted in seven years. Instead, she has repeatedly been an internal entrepreneur and started initiatives which have grown from a start-up team of just four people, to a team of more than 50 people: this is the level of scale where she can see she is making an impact. She has clarity of purpose:

> **The more senior you become, the less you do stuff. At the moment the top people are just focused on layoffs. So there are lots of people who just don't want to be in the executive suite or to be a CEO. They want to do what they enjoy. The more senior you become the less you can do what you want to do and what you enjoy doing. So it is about your priorities. You have to ask who are you doing this for: are you doing it for yourself or for the firm?**

Six months after this interview, she was given an unexpected promotion. She quickly saw the upside of promotion. She discovered that she could have more influence and impact at a higher level, and she could achieve more personal growth:

> **I get much better and more personalised professional development and I get access to executive meetings where decisions are made. Of course, I don't expect to hear about what happens at a global level, but I get to be involved at a local level. Now that I am a director I am invited to different forums, I can understand what is going on and why decisions are made. In the past I had to defend decisions as a manager without knowing why they had been made.**

This transformation neatly captured the dilemma of promotion: at the front line you can see your impact; the more senior you become the more impact you can have, but you cannot see it so directly. Emotionally, the front line is preferable; logically, promotion makes

> **Emotionally, the front line is preferable; logically, promotion makes more sense in terms of impact**

more sense in terms of impact. Logic and emotion come together when you look at managers above you and realise you could do a better job than they can. In the words of one frustrated executive:

> **Often other people get credit for the work I do, and they do not know the nitty gritty of all my work. These are senior executives who will go on stage to talk about the work that we do. They have all the notes that I have given them, and it sounds like they are reading from a script. I am sitting in the audience, and I can see that there is no passion, power or impact in what they are saying, and I realised that I can do it 1,000 times better than they are doing it. So I want to be able to tell the story myself because I think it will be a better story. But I need a bigger title to be invited onto the stage.**

If you can have more impact at a more senior level, and do better than the existing management, then promotion ceases to be about personal ambition: it becomes a moral imperative to support the firm and the mission better. Reframing how you think about promotion matters if you are someone who is not personally ambitious and does not like thrusting yourself into the limelight.

Only you can choose whether you want promotion, either within your firm or by moving between firms. There is no right or wrong answer. It is about what you want to do. If you like working on the front line and using the craft skills you have learned, then keep doing that. The trade-off comes in terms of impact. Your impact will be limited by your lack of formal power, and by the number of hours you can work in a day.

This book is about impact and making things happen through other people: that makes promotion and the acquisition of formal power a very useful tool for you. So the rest of this chapter will focus on four challenges of gaining power and promotion:

1 Invisible rules trump formal rules of promotion, and keep changing.

2 Perspectives and skills change at each level.

3 Expectations change at each level.

4 Create your own secret sauce of success.

1. Invisible rules trump formal rules of promotion, and keep changing

We are surrounded by invisible rules which we obey without thinking about. For instance, what are the rules of a lift? We do not even pause to think that there may be rules of a lift, but we

We are surrounded by invisible rules

still obey the invisible and unwritten rules of using the lift. If someone came into the lift and stood with his back to the doors smiling at everyone, we would be unnerved. We would be even more unnerved if he then greeted each person with a smile, a handshake and a couple of questions such as, 'Good morning, what is your name and how much do you earn?' Very quickly this person would have the lift to himself. If you tried the same approach on the tube, metro or subway you would probably qualify as a member of the Dangerous Sports Club.

The invisible rules revealed themselves when I was with a senior executive from a large Japanese firm. The drink had been flowing, and we had reached the stage of the evening when you can speak the truth and be forgiven (possibly) in the morning. The executive leant over to me and said, 'Owen-san, I have a question for you'. This was the big moment when I would hear the vital truth, so I leaned into him to hear properly. He continued, 'In the West, how do you shake hands?'

What??? How do you shake hands? Isn't that obvious? It may be obvious if you live in the West, but now try explaining it. When do you shake hands, who with, how do you know if and when they are ready to shake hands, how do you signal that you are ready to shake hands, how hard and long should you shake? Suddenly, the Japanese custom of bowing seemed simple: there are clear guidelines about who should bow first, deepest and longest.

Shaking hands and using lifts are trivial examples. Although the rules are invisible, they are well known to most people. The cost of failing to follow the rules is nothing worse than social embarrassment. The cost of failing to follow the invisible rules of work is far higher: it may cost you your career. Here is an example from a professional services firm:

I have seen people fail because they believe the corporate ********. For instance, there were two interns recently. One came from Liverpool and a very modest background. She believed all the corporate spiel about work–life balance. So she was very pleased to be able to leave at 5 o'clock every evening. The other intern came from an aristocratic Spanish high-class background. He understood the invisible rules. He stayed until after everyone else had left. As a result, he got all the interesting work and he got all the support. The Liverpool girl simply did not know the rules. She had to have someone explain to her what the rules really were. She then got it and changed completely.

The invisible rules of promotion are far more complex and have far higher stakes. The big mistake is to trust the formal process.

In theory, the formal process enables the firm to make an objective assessment about who is most suitable for promotion. In practice, the formal process and criteria are not used to make a decision: they are used to justify a decision. In other words, executives make promotion decisions based on invisible rules. They then look at the formal rules and use those criteria to justify their decision and to avoid potential lawsuits. The visible rules give executives the cover they need to make the decisions they want to make. As one

> **The formal process and criteria are not used to make a decision: they are used to justify a decision**

bank executive put it: 'Naturally none of us will challenge the formal HR evaluation criteria. That is not a battle worth fighting. Instead, we all talk about the extra criteria or the special criteria that we are looking for in our area.'

To make the challenge more interesting, the rules change as you progress during your career. These are not rules that you will find in any HR policy framework. Achievement and impact always help, but the informal rules also matter. Here is how they change:

- Early career: promotion on the basis of attitude and potential
- Late career: promotion on the basis of track record, fit and showing you can already do the next job.

Early career: promotion on the basis of attitude and potential

Put yourself in the shoes of a senior executive in a firm with many junior staff. How do you pick out the high potential staff members who can help you make a real impact across the firm? Clearly, you need team members who are reliable and productive. But that tells you little: it only tells you that the team members are good at being junior team members. There will be many team members who pass that low performance threshold. You need some evidence of potential. Time and again senior executives come back to judging people on their attitude and commitment. This often turns out to be a reliable indicator of potential. At the start of your career, you have a limited skill set: mindset is a better predictor of potential.

Mindset is a better predictor of potential

Research and experience consistently show that mindset beats skill set in the early stages of a career. For instance, in a famous test MetLife decided to pit mindset versus skill set in recruiting sales agents. Historically, they had recruited on skill set: they evaluated the aptitude of each candidate. That resulted in a high dropout rate, which was very expensive given the high cost of training each agent. MetLife needed to find a way of picking the right candidates.

For one year, MetLife screened candidates for optimism. They then let the candidates with high optimism scores join, even if they just failed the aptitude test. The results were astonishing. In the first year, the optimists who failed the aptitude test outsold the more skilled recruits by 31 per cent. In year two, the gap grew even larger as the optimists learned their trade: they outsold the traditional recruits by 57 per cent. Optimism screening has now become a standard tool in a range of sales-focused industries, such as real estate. This is not surprising: who wants to buy from, or even work with, a cynical pessimist however skilled they may be?

The importance of attitude in your early career means that you have to manage your brand carefully. In practice, you are unlikely to have much time with senior executives. If you have one bad interaction with a senior executive, that is all that they will remember about you. When they see you are being recommended for promotion, they will start to ask difficult questions about whether you really are ready for promotion. In contrast, if your one interaction with the executive is positive, that will cast a halo of light around your proposed promotion. The executive will not remember what you said, but will remember vividly what you were like. Being positive, optimistic and helpful is a good start. The precise expectations of your manager and other senior executives will be explained in the next section.

How Ms Fairy beat Mr Daz

Jurgen, the CEO, decided to do an unannounced tour of the brand groups in the P&G building. He had started out as a brand manager and he liked to stay in touch with what was being cooked up by each brand group.

I was Mr Daz, responsible for Daz detergent. I was taken by surprise when I turned round and the CEO was standing behind me. He asked how I was and I muttered something about nothing. He moved on to the next cubicle which had Ms Fairy in it: the brand manager for Fairy Liquid. He asked Ms Fairy how

►

she was and she immediately gushed: 'Jurgen, great timing! I am just working on this new promotional idea, I would love to get your advice!' Jurgen beamed with delight: this was his chance to show that the old dog still knew a few tricks.

Twenty minutes later, Jurgen sauntered back to his office feeling he had done a good job, and noting that Ms Fairy was quite a prospect for the future. Unsurprisingly, she was able to get her controversial campaign nodded through in record time because everyone knew the CEO liked it. She also got an early promotion. Meanwhile, I was still struggling to get my more modest campaign approved by all the departments that had to sign it off.

Make the most of every interaction with senior executives, because that is how they will remember you. If a top executive calls by your work station in the next hour, what will you say?

Late career: promotion on the basis of track record, fit and showing you can already do the next job

The rules of survival and success are relatively simple early in your career. They change and become more demanding as you progress. At junior levels, you can be promoted on the basis of attitude and potential: the firm is willing to take a risk on you. If you succeed, that is good for everyone. If you do not succeed, then there is little loss to the firm and there are always plenty of other people who can fill your shoes.

At senior levels, the process becomes much more risk averse. The consequences of making a bad appointment are much higher. Ideally, the firm will appoint someone who is already doing the job even if they have not got the title. What this means in practice for you:

a) Doing a good job in your current role is not enough.

b) Find the right experiences and assignments.

c) Have a claim to fame and stake your claim.

d) Mind your brand.

a) *Doing a good job in your current role is not enough.* Many of your peers will also be doing a good job, so that is not a distinctive claim to fame. But even if you are one of the highest performers at your current level, that simply proves you are at the right level. It does not show that you can do the job one level up.

> **Doing a good job in your current role is not enough**

b) *Find the right experiences and assignments.* Prove that you can do everything that is required at the level you aspire to. You may get lucky with the formal assignment process and gain the right experience. But luck is not a strategy. You need to create your own opportunities. You can do this in three ways:

- Use your sponsor to help identify and guide you to the right assignments: informal power supports formal power.

- Crises are a great opportunity to step up when others are stepping back into the safety of the shadows.

- Volunteer for new initiatives or difficult initiatives which others are hesitant to take on. Volunteering not only gives you good experience, it often gives you good visibility with senior executives.

Have you got what it takes?

Fatima Koumbarji, long-term partner at search firm Odgers, was responsible for recruiting at the most senior levels in higher education for positions such as vice chancellor. Here is the view from the other side of the table about what you need to succeed:

'You have to get some experience of working and delivering at the next level to show that you can operate at the next

➤

level. It can feel unfair if you are being paid at the lower level to do a higher level job. But you have to prove yourself first or demonstrate your potential with relevant examples. If I am recruiting someone, I want to know that they will hit the ground running as that is what my clients expect. I don't expect to tell them how to do the job, especially at a senior level, but I will assess them against the challenges facing the role.

I interviewed someone for a position as a vice chancellor at a university. They were operating as a dean of a large faculty. I needed assurance that they can operate across the university, not just within their own faculty. They have to show that they can work in a multi-disciplinary way with social scientists and engineers and health professionals. You can do that by volunteering for projects which cut across the university and make an impact. It is useless if you just sit on a committee. You have to put your hand up: you have to lead something. If you volunteer, you get the opportunity to lead because an extra pair of hands is always welcome. It is important to play to your strengths and interests.

You have to have the confidence to step up. You have to do the research: has someone actually thought themselves into the role?

Why do some people not get promoted? Often it can be because they scare the pants off people. They can be too honest or too abrasive or too quirky. Then the selection committee fears that this person is going to turn everything upside down without actually understanding their needs.

It's also about values. Are they aligned and what is the actual evidence that they have those values?'

c) *Have a claim to fame and stake your claim.* You know you are doing a good job, but does anyone else know or believe that? Your

Have a claim to fame and stake your claim

peers are also doing a good job. They are probably building the experience to show that they can work at the next level. Can you stand out? We have already seen that if you want to have impact you need a distinctive claim to fame, such as organising the corporate presence at UNGA. Sometimes, the claim to fame is so distinctive and high profile that it markets itself, especially if the CEO is involved as at UNGA.

More usually, you will find that it is not enough to work hard, take risks and have a claim to fame: you need to stake your claim. You need to make sure everyone else knows about your success, without appearing to be a jerk who claims all the credit and annoys everyone else who has contributed. In Chapter 1 we saw that a good way to claim the credit is to give it away. Be generous with your praise. Colleagues will appreciate your generosity, and recognise that the praise giver must have been the leader of the effort: you claim the credit by appearing to give it away.

Communicating success is how you gain permission to keep doing what you are doing. If no one realises that you are doing something valuable then you have a problem. Perceptions may be false, but the consequences of those perceptions are always real. Manage perceptions, even if that takes some creativity, as the case below shows.

Building your claim to fame

Ed Beckingham is responsible for learning and development of managers and high potentials at Barratt Redrow, a major housebuilder with an annual turnover exceeding £5 billion. He developed a programme that successfully doubled the number of female leaders participating. The key innovation was allowing candidates to nominate themselves, rather than being nominated by managing directors. While this change initially caused some concern, it ensured greater candidate commitment and engagement.

➤

Ed skilfully communicated the programme's success to the MDs, despite the challenge that many MDs manage teams of over 200 people: knowing everyone and their aspirations in detail is a challenge. He explains:

'There were 29 managing directors with people on the programme. I personalised each email to highlight the positive impact of the programme, rather than sending out a bulk email. We used delegates' full names in each email so that each managing director would recognise who I was talking about. I would not simply refer to their first name; I would give their full name to ensure recognition. Then, I included three follow-up questions or actions for each participant. This allowed the managing director to ask relevant questions and have meaningful conversations about the programme. I aimed to help the managing directors connect with the programme and the delegates.'

Ed was not selling, bragging or boasting. He made connections so that each MD could have a practical conversation with their participants. He let the participants sell the programme to the MDs themselves.

d) *Mind your brand*. Kenji Ota is the CEO of Zurich Life in Japan and he recognises the importance of brand. Occasionally he meets up with former executives of a major Japanese trading company. 'All I have to do is just give them the name of someone and I will always get the same reply from everyone even if they have left the firm 10 years ago or worked in a different division. They might say this one is handsome and don't trust him around women. Or they might say he's the one that created an inventory problem which took us five years to shift. The feedback is remarkably consistent about the name-dropped person. So, everyone knows your brand. People with a good brand get lots of support.'

Formal HR systems can record your performance appraisals, but that is weak compared to the reputation you build. Just as you discuss colleagues around the water cooler, where judgements are often simple and not always positive, so you will be the topic of discussion around the water cooler, at the bar or at the club. You have no way of knowing where or when those discussions take place or what will be said, but they are the conversations that can shape your fate.

Japan may be an outlier with its longer term employment patterns. But your brand still matters wherever you are. You build it up over time. Here is Kenji again: 'You never know when you will need help so it is better to be a giver than a taker. Of course, some people can succeed in the short term by being a taker, but eventually their reputation catches up with them.'

It is easy to spot the executives who are trying to burnish their brand at the last moment to gain promotion. One bank requires its executives to do some voluntary work outside the bank to reach MD level: I am regularly inundated with applications to become trustees of a charity around promotion time from this bank. It is very transparent, and it does not fool the charity or the bank. Another bank requires MD candidates to show that they are mentoring or supporting the next generation. About nine months before decisions are made, candidates suddenly start scheduling breakfast meetings with junior staff. Then they are surprised that no one takes them seriously.

Building your brand is a long-term exercise where you have to be consistent about what you do and how you do it. For a moment,

Building your brand is a long-term exercise

think about how you would like a senior executive to describe you at the tennis club. What have you done to demonstrate your brand to that person? You know how you want to be seen, but proving it is far harder.

2. Perspectives and skills change at each level

What got you here will not get you there. Having impact as a new graduate working as a junior member of a team is very different from having

What got you here will not get you there

impact as a CEO. You have to learn new skills and adapt as you progress. This is both a risk and an opportunity for you.

The risk is that you stick with the success formula which gained your first promotion. Imagine that you are the best player on your soccer team. You do so well that you are appointed team manager. Delighted with this vote of confidence in your ability, you decide to double down on what made you successful. You now run twice as hard, make twice as many tackles and attempt to score more goals. You are then fired, and you wonder what went wrong. Your job as team coach is not to run around the pitch making all the tackles and scoring all the goals. Your goal is to select the team, train the team and manage the tactics and competitive strategy. It is a completely different job which you have to learn.

Many first-time leaders are like the soccer-player-turned-manager: they do not realise how much their job has changed and they struggle greatly. Promotion is a moment of great triumph and great peril in your career.

Promotion is a moment of great triumph and great peril in your career

Your opportunity comes from understanding how the world will change as you progress. The table below tells your future better than any fortune teller with the best crystal ball in the world.

Your evolving career

Perspective	Entry level	Top level
Key skills	Technical: learn your trade	People and political skills
Time horizon	Today, this week, this month	From today to five years out
Agenda	React to the agenda given to you	Create the agenda for others to follow
Risk appetite	High: experiment and learn	Low: make your numbers
Key question	How can I do this?	Who can do this?
Focus	Manage self	Manage others
View	Detail at the bottom of the mountain	Big picture, strategy from the top of the mountain
Promotion criteria	Perceived attitude, plus performance	Demonstrate you can do the next job; have a claim to fame
Tenure with employer	2–3 years average	10–15 years average

Once you know the future, you can prepare for it. Take a look at the top-level perspective. You can start to work on these skills and perspectives today. The more you understand the top-level perspective, the easier it is for you to engage with the top level. You will understand them and they will understand you. You will find it far easier to sell your agenda to them and to have impact; they will find it far easier to promote you so that you can have even more impact.

Here are four perspectives you can develop at any stage of your career, which will help you now and in the future:

- *Create the agenda.* You do not have to wait until you reach the corner office to start creating the agenda. You can start creating it now. We saw how Amanda Timberg created the global apprenticeship programme at Google, and Tia Lendo created the campaign to get Chromebooks into schools. These were not initiatives that were ordered from on high. They saw the need and the opportunity and they made it happen. There are always unmet needs and opportunities.

- *Think big.* It is very easy to get lost in the swamp and focus on the details and today's urgent deadline. Top management want you to look after that detail, and most of the time they will assume that you are in control. But if you want to get noticed, you have to go to them with something which makes a difference to the big picture. Understand the direction they want to go and help them, or show them that there is another opportunity they can take. The bigger it is, the more they will take notice. As we have already seen, if you want to start a bank or start the largest graduate recruiter in the UK, you can do it. The smallest obstacles are rational and strategic; the middle-sized obstacles are people and politics and the selling process; the biggest obstacle is usually in our heads. We cover this in Chapter 8.

- *Risk appetite.* This is where entry-level staff have an advantage over senior staff. Senior management normally become more risk averse: they have to make their numbers if they are to survive. At more junior levels, you can take more risk. You are more likely to be forgiven if the risk goes bad for three reasons:

> **At more junior levels, you can take more risk**

  - Taking a risk shows initiative and shows potential.
  - Most managers are forgiving: they have been in your shoes and know that not everything works out every time.

- At junior levels, the risks are normally smaller and the costs of failure are also small: it is easier to be forgiving.

If things go horribly wrong, it is far easier to start again when you are 25 than when you are 45 with a mortgage and college fees to pay. Take risks and learn at speed while you can.

- *Build your people and political skills.* If you create the agenda, think big and take risks, you will need to build the people and political skills to deliver your agenda. You will be learning the PQ skills that enable you to amplify your impact wherever you are in the organisation. You will also be learning the skills you need to progress to greater levels of responsibility. Your learning journey can start at any time, but the earlier the better.

3. Expectations change at each level

I have asked many leaders what makes a good leader. The answer is normally guff. They do not describe leadership; they describe an idealised version of themselves. After some years of asking the wrong question, I finally found two more insightful questions:

- What do you expect of your leader?
- What do you expect of your team members?

I have asked these two questions thousands of times, and the answers are now more or less predictable. The answers reveal what is really expected of you at every level, regardless of the formal evaluation criteria. This is how you will be judged in practice; the formal HR criteria will simply be used to justify a decision based on these more informal criteria. As ever, the informal system beats the formal system.

Expectations of what makes a good leader change by level
(Satisfaction ratings in brackets against each expectation)

Entry-level team members	Leaders in the middle	Senior leaders
Hard work (64%)	Ability to motivate others (43%)	Vision (61%)
Proactivity (57%)	Decisiveness (54%)	Ability to motivate others (37%)
Intelligence (63%)	Industry experience (70%)	Decisiveness (47%)
Reliability (61%)	Networking ability (57%)	Ability to handle crises (56%)
Ambition (64%)	Delegation (43%)	Honesty and integrity (48%)

The table above is full of small words with big meanings, which can be explored at another time. From the perspective of impact and careers, the vital takeaways are:

- Expectations change at every level. You have to keep on learning and adapting your success model to survive.

- Expectations are minimally related to formal performance or promotion criteria; these expectations will shape how you are perceived and rated.

- Early in your career you will be judged mainly on your attitude; later, your skills become more important.

- Satisfaction with performance against these criteria is low. Typically, 50–65 per cent are satisfied with colleagues on each criterion. You do not have to be a genius to stand out against your colleagues.

As ever, we judge ourselves by our intentions and others by their actions. We know in our hearts that we perform well

As ever, we judge ourselves by our intentions and others by their actions

against all these criteria, especially on a good day. But the test is not about how you think you perform on a good day. The test is how others think you perform, especially on difficult days. If you are positive, pro-active and decisive on good days, but then disappear without trace in a crisis, or you become angry and upset, then you will be remembered for that one day out of one hundred when things went awry.

4. Create your own secret sauce of success

If there was a universal success formula, someone would have found it by now and would have made a fortune. The universal success formula is like the elixir of eternal life: it has not been found, and never will be. This is good news. If there was a universal formula for success, we would have all been replaced by an algorithm. There is a good reason why no universal formula exists:

- Contexts vary by culture and by industry. What works in a Silicon Valley start-up is different from what works in a large Japanese multinational, which is different from what works in the French civil service, for instance.

- You are unique and your colleagues are unique. The average human being is 51 per cent female and has slightly less than two legs and two eyes: accurate, but useless because the average never describes the person in front of you.

- Every situation is unique. There are inevitable patterns to every crisis, to every new product launch and every change programme. Understanding the patterns gives clues to what works and what does not work, but you still have to adapt to the reality which is staring you in the face.

- Everything is changing all the time. Greek philosopher Heraclitus wrote, over 2,000 years ago: 'You cannot step in the same river twice' because the river is always changing. Your firm, your colleagues, your situation change far faster than any river. To update Heraclitus: you cannot do the same job twice.

If you have to create your own magic sauce of success, the big question is, 'How?' I have asked countless executives in workshops how they have learned to have impact and to lead. To make it

> **You have to create your own magic sauce of success**

simple, I let them choose two main sources of learning from six possible sources. Decide which are the two most useful sources of learning for you:

- books;
- courses;
- bosses (good and bad lessons);
- peers and colleagues;
- role models (beyond work);
- personal experience.

Virtually no one chooses books or courses, which could be bad news for an author who delivers courses for a living. Quite a few hands vote in favour of observed experience, and a forest of hands erupt when it comes to personal experience. This makes good sense. When you see someone do something which works, try to copy it. If you see them blow up, make a quiet note not to repeat that mistake. Learning from observed and personal experience is highly practical: it helps you discover what works for you in your context.

But there are three problems with learning from experience:

- *Experience is a slow way to learn.* 'Experience' can be used as an excuse for keeping junior managers junior until they have put in the years required. It is a good way of stopping you from progressing your career.

- *Experience can be painful for you and your colleagues.* Trial and error is fine when it works; it is not fine when it does not work.

- *Experience is a random walk.* If you happen to get good bosses, colleagues and assignments you learn the right lessons and you accelerate your career. If you are unlucky with your bosses, colleagues and assignments you may be careering into a dead end.

A random walk is not a good way to manage your career. You need a better way. This is where books and courses can help. You will not be able to read a book and finish it on page 191 as the

> **A random walk is not a good way to manage your career**

perfect leader. But books and courses help you make sense of the nonsense you encounter and can help structure and accelerate your learning journey. They support your learning, but do not replace it.

The best way to discover your unique magic sauce is to make sure you get the right bosses, colleagues and assignments. Once again, your informal network is better for you than the formal HR process. Your network and your sponsor should give you early warning of where the best managers need help and where the best assignments are emerging. They should also let you know when the Death Star projects with Darth Vader-type managers are looking for victims to staff their project. Armed with the right information you can either make yourself very busy and unavailable, or you can suddenly discover that you have some discretionary time to volunteer some help on an emerging project. Possession is nine-tenths of the law: if you have helped a manager shape an idea, the chances are that you will be invited to help deliver the idea. The formal assignment process will eventually catch up and confirm the informal agreement you have reached.

Summary

So far, you have discovered the tool set and skill set you need to have impact at any level, and how you can grow your formal and informal power. But there is one more magic ingredient of success that the highest impact managers have. They not only have the right skill set, they all have the right mindset. Fortunately, these habits of minds are universal and anyone can learn them. That is the focus of the final chapter which follows.

chapter 8

Raise your inner game

Look around your office and you will find some colleagues greatly outperform others, even although they have similar skill sets. The difference is mindset, which eats skill set for breakfast. The good news is that anyone can learn the habits of mind for success. This chapter shows how.

Mindset versus skill set

Every leader is flawed. This is great news. No leader gets ticks in all the boxes, which means that you do not need ticks in all the boxes. You do not need to be perfect to succeed. Flaws do not disappear over time: they appear to grow. When you live in the shadows of the organisation, any minor flaws you have will be picked up as 'development opportunities' by your manager. Do not worry too much about these perceived flaws. No one ever succeeded by working on their weaknesses. You would not tell an Olympic weightlifter to address their relative weakness in synchronised swimming. Focus on your strengths: they will carry you to where you want to go to.

> **No leader gets ticks in all the boxes**

> **You do not need to be perfect to succeed**

Your minor flaws appear to grow as you move out of the shadows and into the spotlight of leadership because everyone is looking at you much more closely. Many of these flaws simply do not matter. If you hate accounting, learn to love accountants: leadership is a team sport and you do not need to be good at everything.

For 20 years I worked with and researched some of the most outstanding leaders in the world to understand what particular skill set a leader needs. Slowly, I realised that there is no universal formula. Each leader has a unique skill set which works where they work. You have to find the match between your strengths and where you work. If there is a good fit, you will fly. If there is no fit, you will struggle.

If skills do not define success, what does?

The answer appeared at the end of an interview with a CEO. He relaxed and blurted out a truth: 'I find I hire most people for their skills, and fire most for how they are (values and mindset)'. Very few people are fired because they lack the skills for the job. They leave because they have the wrong mindset and values.

> **I hire most people for their skills, and fire most for how they are**

There is a good reason for this: firms can train skill set, but not mindset. Although the firm cannot develop your mindset, you can. Mindset is not

Firms can train skill set, but not mindset

like your genes which you cannot change. Instead, think of mindset as 'habits of mind'. We all have habits which help us get through the day, and we all have some habits which can hold us back. It is the same with habits of mind: they help us or hinder us. As with all habits, you can learn new habits, control unhelpful habits and perhaps eliminate other habits. Learning new habits is like learning a language, a musical instrument or a sport: it takes time and effort. But even a little effort maintained consistently over time can make a big difference.

Recruiting: mindset or skill set?

Timpson runs a chain of shoe repair shops across the UK. Most shops are small and run by one or two people. They repair shoes, engrave trophies and cut keys. Staff are modestly paid. For many years, Timpson recruited cobblers because they had the skills required for the job. And for many years, this proved costly in terms of staff turnover and customer satisfaction.

Timpson then did something radical. He decided to recruit to values, not to skills. He reasoned that you can train skills, but not values. To make the point, he gave all his area managers a sheet of paper populated by cartoon characters. On one side was Mrs Happy, Mr Friendly, Mr Helpful, Mrs Honest, Mr Keen. On the other side was Mr Scruffy, Ms Late, Mr Rude, Miss Fib, Mr Can't do, Mrs Slow. This became the basis of recruiting.

The results have helped Timpson dominate its market because he recruits people who want to do a good job and help customers. He then trains them in the skills they need. It means he has been able to recruit from unlikely sources: he is a leading recruiter of ex-offenders, for instance.

Mindset eats skill set for breakfast.

For the last ten years, my research has shown that there are seven positive habits of mind which enable success, plus one mindset from the dark side. There are also a series of mindset traps which stop anyone succeeding. The traps come in the form of stories we tell ourselves. Here are the seven plus one mindsets of impact, and the eight mindset traps which this chapter explores:

Impact mindsets	Mindset traps
High aspirations	Just work hard and I will succeed
Courage	I don't have the experience
Resilience	I don't have the power
Positive	I don't have the resources
Collaborative	I don't belong
Accountable	I am not good enough
Growth	I must not fail
Ruthlessness	Politics is a dirty business and not for me

Eight impact mindsets

1. High aspirations

This is the most important of all the mindsets. If you have low aspirations, you will achieve little. High aspirations is not a mysterious mindset that you are either born with or not. You will have high aspirations as soon as you find a mission which you believe in and you are committed to. Find your mission, find your purpose and you will quickly acquire the mindset of success.

High aspirations matter for four reasons. It helps you:

- *Unlock all the other mindsets.* If you have a mission you truly believe in, you will find the courage to do things you would not normally do; you will discover that you have the resilience to bounce back from setbacks; you will be relentlessly positive; you will seek out partners to collaborate with and make it happen; you will take responsibility and you will quickly learn and grow. You will also discover that you have a ruthless streak: you will have the difficult conversations and make the difficult decisions to ensure you achieve your mission.

- *Show ambition.* Managers want team members who are ambitious, as we saw in Chapter 1. They want team members who are ambitious for the team and for the mission. They want you to make a difference and put in the discretionary effort required.

- *Gain power and visibility within your organisation.* If you have a clear and distinctive agenda, you will gain the attention, support and possibly opposition. But you will not be ignored. You will have opened the door to having impact and making more happen.

> **If you have a clear and distinctive agenda, you will gain the attention, support and possibly opposition**

- *Find purpose and meaning in your work.* When you own your work, the productivity mindset follows naturally. Equally naturally you will find yourself learning to hustle effectively and make things happen.

2. Courage

It is not enough to have ambition. You have to dare to act as well. If you want to make a difference and have impact, you will be challenging and changing the existing ways. That in itself takes courage because you know you will face obstacles and resistance. You have to take risks.

> **Dare to act**

There are two ways you can learn courage. I discovered in my work with the fire service, special forces and mountaineers that they all learn courage, and they all learn it the same way: one step at a time, with professional coaching and support. If you want to conquer the highest and toughest peaks, do not simply book your flight to the Himalayas and hope for the best. Start with the simplest tasks: learning to camp out safely, perhaps starting in your backyard. Progress to hill walking, then tackling small climbs. Slowly increase the difficulty of the climbs and the conditions with support from more experienced climbers; eventually, the highest peaks will become possible even if they are never easy.

The alternative way is to jump into the deep end of the pool: find your mission and go for it. This is scary and exhilarating. Fortunately, if it goes wrong you will not lose your life, unlike the mountaineers, special forces and fire service. You will find that you are living life with the record button on, and in full technicolor. You will learn faster than you ever thought possible before. Once again, having a clear mission drives the right habits of mind.

3. Resilience

Resilience flows from courage. Courage is about taking risks, and risk carries the risk of failure. If you have never failed, you have never pushed yourself far enough and never taken enough risk. In the words of poet William Blake:

You never know what is enough unless you know what is more than enough.

(Proverbs of Hell)

Like courage, you can build resilience over time. The more you learn to deal with the tough stuff and with setbacks, the easier they are to deal with: you become more resilient and more effective. In practice, resilience is often the product of other habits of mind:

- High aspirations: a deep sense of purpose and mission will drive you to overcome obstacles and setbacks.

- Positive mindset is not about hoping to get lucky. It is about keeping the end in mind; finding solutions, driving to action and never doubting that you will prevail. These habits will help you find your natural resilience.

- Collaborative: a problem shared is a problem halved and a joy shared is a joy doubled. Find the personal and professional support you need in hard times. Don't carry the burdens of the world on your own back. Share the burden and you can bounce back.

A problem shared is a problem halved and a joy shared is a joy doubled

- Growth mindset does not treat setbacks as failure. The growth mindset uses every challenge to learn more, come back stronger and get one step closer to success

4. Positive

You cannot tell people to be positive, happy or motivated. These things come from within. In practice, we all have days when we are positive, happy and motivated and we also have days when we struggle. Good days and bad days are not random: they come from creating the conditions where you will thrive (see the case study below).

You cannot tell people to be positive, happy or motivated

Even on bad days, you have to learn to wear the mask of leadership. Leaders are purveyors of hope, clarity and optimism, especially when there seems to be none. As one CEO put it: 'Treat every day as the first night of the show. Always bring your best self to the stage.' If you come in with your little cloud of gloom, that will quickly spread like a major depression across your team. And if you are not positive, no one else will be positive for you.

Leaders are purveyors of hope, clarity and optimism, especially when there seems to be none

Motivating millions of people

For the last 13 years STIR Education (where I am founding chair) has been working out how to build motivation at scale. It is now working with seven million officials, teachers and students in six countries. It has found that people are naturally positive and motivated if four conditions are in place, which follow a simple acronym: RAMP.

- **R**elationships which are positive and supportive, both vertically (with your managers and team members) and laterally (with your peers). Toxic workplaces are just that: toxic, which makes it hard to stay positive.

- **A**utonomy, because professionals have pride and do not like being micromanaged. Learn to trust your peers and team. They will usually repay your trust by delivering for you.

- **M**astery, because it is hard to feel positive or motivated if you do not have the skills for today's role and you are not building the skills for tomorrow's role. Learning is in itself motivating.

- **P**urpose: having a sense of mission and purpose is energising and makes even mundane work have relevance. Find the right agenda to work on.

If you can find the conditions where RAMP exists for you, you will discover your intrinsic motivation and positive outlook. If you create RAMP for your own team, you will have a positive and motivated team which performs well.

5. Collaborative

When you move from being a team member to being a team leader, you have to change how you think about tasks. Instead of asking 'how can I do this?' you need to ask 'who can do this?' The shift from 'how' to 'who' is

Instead of asking 'how can I do this?' you need to ask 'who can do this?'

profound, and is at the heart of this book. The way you have impact and do more with less is by doing things through other people. Collaboration is at the heart of amplifying your personal impact.

You cannot be collaborative unless others trust you and you trust others. Trust is a two-way street. There is no point in diligently earning the trust of your peers if you cannot trust them. It

Trust is a two-way street

is lack of trust which makes many managers poor at delegation. As soon as you delegate a task, you create risk by becoming dependent on someone else. Managers have many excuses for not delegating such as:

- This is too important.
- It is quicker for me to do it than to delegate it.
- It is too difficult for the team, so I must do it.

Each excuse can be translated very simply: 'I don't trust my team.' If you don't trust your team, either you have the wrong team or your team has the wrong manager.

6. Accountable

Accountability sounds very boring, but it is not. It is part of the magic sauce that frees you from the gilded cage of your firm's hierarchy, processes and procedures. It transforms you from being dependent on events to controlling and influencing events. You cease to be a victim of fate; instead, you control your destiny.

Clearly, the firm does not let you control everything. But you can influence whatever you choose to influence. The accountable mindset means that you:

a)   control what you can;

b)   influence what you cannot control directly;

c)   plan contingencies for what you can neither control nor influence.

a) *Control what you can* sounds obvious, but takes high-impact managers much further than average managers. For them, accountability results in two important behaviours:

- Own your work and your out-comes, which drives the productivity mindset. High-impact managers constantly

> **Own your work and your outcomes**

referred to how they 'get s**t done'. They cannot imagine failing to deliver on time. The ownership mindset also means they own, and overcome, any obstacles in their way. They do not behave like disempowered junior staff.

- Control your emotions and how you present yourself to your team. Don't let others, or events, dictate your feelings: that way, your emotions become vic-tims of circumstance. You can

> **Don't let others, or events, dictate your feelings**

choose how you react to events. This is a liberating discovery, although very hard to learn and to apply. In the words of Fiona Dawson, chair of the Chartered Management Institute: 'especially in a crisis, you have to import stress and export seren-ity'. Another senior executive put it more bluntly: 'Authenticity is not being authentically stupid, it is about being the best of who you are.' Choose wisely when you choose your emotions and how to present yourself to the world.

b) *Influence what you cannot control*. For instance, you cannot con-trol the narrative about how you are perceived. We saw from the tale of the tennis club where senior executives discussed, and trashed, the reputation of staff that your reputation precedes you. The accountable mindset understands this and works hard to influence perceptions:

- Celebrating and sharing successes widely.

- Creating a clear narrative about how setbacks were success-fully overcome.

- Having a sponsor or sponsors who will be in the room rooting for you when you are discussed behind your back.

c) *Plan contingencies for what you can neither control nor influence.* For instance, you cannot control whether your firm will be hit by a crisis which threatens its existence. Today's titans often turn out to be yesterday's also-rans. Firms on average survive in the S&P 500 for just 21 years; only 27 of the original FTSE 100 firms in 1983 are still there. The accountable mindset recognises that you can no longer rely on your employer for long-term employment: you have to build your employability. That means:

> **Build your employability**

- *Keep your skills up to date*: you need to compete with people who may be younger, hungrier, cheaper and with more current skills.
- *Maintain your network and manage your industry profile*: most roles are sourced through networks, not through advertising.
- *Demonstrate that you can make a real impact*: have a claim to fame.

7. Growth

Much has been written about the growth mindset, and rightly so. You have to keep changing and adapting to new roles, new technology, new circumstances, new employers, new competition. Growth and learning are to be enjoyed, not endured. Both mastery and the journey to mastery is intrinsically rewarding.

Hokusai epitomises the joy of the mastery journey. His print of the *Great Wave* adorns T-shirts, tea towels and mugs around the world. Here he writes about learning: 'Nothing I produced before the age of 70 is worthy of note. Not until I was 73 did I begin to understand the structure of nature as it truly is, the structure of animals, plants, trees, birds, fish and insects. Thus, by the time I am 80, I will have made some real progress. At 90 I will have fathomed the mystery of things; at 100 I will surely have reached a phenomenal level.'

In a 40-year career, you will have to reinvent yourself several times. Imagine the world 40 years ago: it was a world without internet or mobile phones; the PC was an exotic item for enthusiasts; social media and many of the world's top firms today did not exist or were minnows. No one can predict what the world will look like in another 40 years, other than it will be very different from today.

> **In a 40-year career, you will have to reinvent yourself several times**

The skills you have today will not be enough to sustain you for 40 years. You have to keep learning, keep changing, keep adapting. Enjoy the ride.

> **Keep learning, keep changing, keep adapting**

Change or die

I have spent 15 years working with and researching tribes and traditional societies around the world. From Mali to Mongolia, the Arctic to Australia and Papua New Guinea and beyond, there is one simple message: change or die. Everyone has to learn new ways of living and surviving.

At first this seems unlikely. Tribes can seem like living fossils which have not changed in thousands of years. But closer examination shows that every tribe either wants to change or has to change. For instance:

- In the Highlands of Papua New Guinea the village chief bought a mobile phone and solar panel charger for the village. They now check the price of coffee on the London market, invite bids from nearby markets for their crop and then go with the highest bidder. The village income has doubled as a result.

- In southern Ethiopia, the arrival of Kalashnikovs has changed everything. A tribal arms race is underway both for protecting the tribe and raiding other tribes.

- In the Arctic, global warming is changing the migration patterns of the reindeer which the Saami depend on in Norway; in Finland, land rights and EU farm policies means that the reindeer migration has stopped and the Saami become settled farmers.

- The Laikipia in northern Kenya have turned from killing animals to caring for animals: four years of drought made them realise that if the animals die, they would die as well.

- The Hadza in Tanzania are one of the last hunter-gatherer tribes in the world. They are threatened by population growth which means that neighbouring tribes are encroaching on their territory. It is unclear how they will survive.

- In Mali the Dogon had no litter. As subsistence farmers they have no money to buy things to throw away. But they want to buy a village television and radio, and a motorbike to communicate with the outside world. They want to move from subsistence farming to cash crops. Their culture will change dramatically as a result.

If tribes have to change, then firms have to change even faster, and executives have to change faster again. You cannot change unless you learn, adapt and grow. Growth is survival: change or die.

8. Ruthlessness

Ruthlessness is the mindset from the dark side. Every leader I interview objects to being described as ruthless, but would then go on to admit that they needed a hard edge.

Ruthlessness comes from high aspirations. If you have a very clear mission and you are committed to it, you will do what it takes to achieve that mission. You will find the courage to have the difficult conversation and to make the difficult decision. You will not do this because you are a psychopath who delights in wrecking lives and careers. You will do it because the mission comes first.

Ruthlessness is not about being nasty. If you are clear about the goal, be flexible about the means. Support the team and recognise that the best way to achieve your goal may not be to go in a straight line: when you are sailing against the wind you have to learn to zig zag. However flexible you are about the means, the ruthless leader is not flexible about the goal. If you decide to climb the mountain, climb the mountain: fishing in the valley may be nicer, but is not going to get you to the top of the mountain.

If you have a soft edge, not a hard edge, you will be popular but ineffective. You will understand why a deadline needs to be put back, why a target needs to be reduced and why a budget will not be met. When you accept excuses, you accept failure.

> **When you accept excuses, you accept failure**

Hard edged or ruthless?

Two trainee teachers joined the school at the same time. Their careers and personal lives progressed in parallel. They became good friends. Even after they both started families, their families would go on holiday together and occasionally have Sunday lunch together. In time, both became heads of department.

Eventually, one of them was chosen to become head teacher. She was ambitious to improve the school, and to enhance the life prospects of children who attended the school. She realised that there was one department which was stopping progress: the English department. English language is a gateway subject: if children do not master the language, they cannot master any other subjects. It was clear to the head teacher that the head of English had to go. The head of English also happened to be the friend that had started with her at the school 20 years previously.

> The new head teacher fired her long-term friend. That was an end of the friendship, the holidays and the Sunday lunches. The future lives of hundreds of children mattered more than one friendship.
>
> Hard edged, or ruthless?

Eight mindset traps

1. Just work hard and I will succeed

School also teaches you that hard work means you will succeed. This is only partly true. Achieving high impact is hard work physically and emotionally. Walter Emberger talks for many entrepreneurs when he describes how he felt when starting Teach for Austria, in the face of very powerful opposition: 'It was physically hard and when I talk about it I feel pain in my stomach. It was worst on Sunday evenings when I realised there were all these balls to juggle next week and I had to decide which balls I had to keep juggling and which balls I had to let drop. That was very hard.'

Working hard matters, but is never enough. If you want to succeed and have impact, you have to work smart, not just hard. That means:

Working hard matters, but is never enough

You have to work smart, not just hard

- *Work on the right agenda.* You need to find promotable work, as well as regular work. If you always volunteer to take minutes, you will work hard and be seen as a minute taker, not a change maker. High-impact managers don't just accept the assignments given to them. They work the informal networks of the firm to find the right assignment. When the chance arises, they will create a new agenda in response to a crisis or opportunity.

- *Find the right sponsors* who have your back when it matters. They need to be rooting for you when you are not in the room and promotions, bonuses and assignments are being discussed; they are the people who will warn you of hazards ahead and help you overcome political obstacles. They are your fairy godmother or godfather of impact and career progress.

- *Control the narrative* about how you are seen. Manage your brand internally. This is about how you behave and how you perform: how you are and what you do. You also have to manage your messaging. You know what you do, but do not expect everyone else to know because they have many other things to worry about.

- *Make the most of each interaction with top executives.* If you are presenting to them, overinvest in making it a great presentation. If you are in a meeting with them, make sure you have a good contribution to make. Silence is not golden: it shows that you have nothing worthwhile to say and you should not be there. Even be ready for the accidental meeting: what will you say if you bump into the CEO in the corridor? These small interactions will define how you are perceived, rightly or wrongly.

2. I don't have the experience

Telling team members that they need more experience is a good way of keeping junior people junior until they have served their time. In the past, the leader was expected to be the most experienced and smartest person in the room. That is no longer true. Your job is not to be the smartest and most experienced person on the team: your job is to bring the smartest and most experienced people onto your team. Look at the ages when ten of today's top tech billionaires started their firms:

> **Your job is not to be the smartest and most experienced person on the team**

- Mark Zuckerberg, Facebook: 19 years old
- Michael Dell, Dell computers: 19 years old
- Bill Gates, Microsoft: 20 years old

- Steve Jobs, Apple: 21 years old
- Elon Musk, first start-up Zip2 at age 24. Sold for $307 million four years later.
- Sergey Brin, Google: 25 years old
- Larry Page, Google: 26 years old
- Jeff Bezos, Amazon: 30 years old
- Jensen Huang, Nvidia: 30 years old
- Larry Ellison, Oracle: 33 years old

If you want to become a tech billionaire, you may be over the hill after the age of 30. If you have a great idea, you can build a team with great experience to turn your idea into impact. You are as experienced as the team you build.

3. I don't have the power

Have you ever heard of someone complaining that they have too much power? The way organisations work is that your responsibilities always exceed your formal authority. The essence of *Impact* is to show how you can amplify your formal power by building up your informal power. You have to make things happen through people you do not control.

Chapter 1 showed that you can acquire four types of informal power:

- *Referent power*: become the trusted colleague that people want to work with, rather than the one they have to work with.

- *Agenda power*: make the agenda, don't take it. Find the big idea which gives you meaning and purpose, and power and visibility across the organisation.

- *Expert power*: you have a skill which is in demand, otherwise you would not be in work. Keep learning and growing, because the expertise you need changes over your career.

- *Information*: you have insight and perspectives that others do not have. Knowledge is power.

Use these sources of power well and you will be able to find the resources, secure the support and get the budget you need to make things happen. No one ever has enough formal power: the difference is that some people are able to amplify their formal power with their four sources of informal power. Other people are left complaining that they do not have enough power, and that becomes an excuse for underachievement.

4. I don't have the resources

No one complains about having too much power, and no one complains about having too much resource. The resource challenge is normal because the corporate world is forever engaged in the sport called betterfastercheaper. You have four ways of addressing the resource challenge:

- *Work harder.* This is the response of naïve managers. They work longer and harder to meet impossible deadlines and targets. This is heroic, occasionally necessary and completely unsustainable.

- *Work smarter*: find better and cheaper ways of achieving the same outcome. Challenge what you are doing and how you are doing it. There are normally shortcuts. For most problems, someone else has probably already worked on a similar problem and has at least part of the solution for you. For instance, every time I start a new charity there is the predictable challenge of creating an employee handbook, creating the right financial controls and HR policies and procedures. It is a huge task which no start-up team can afford. There is a simple solution: borrow all the policies, procedures and handbooks from another charity and adapt them: 90 per cent of the work is avoided.

- *Challenge the outcome*: what is the real goal, who needs it, what do they need and what is the minimum viable product? For instance, P&G had a costly problem. Every year, they had to hire a steeple-jack to climb the factory chimney to check that the cowling at the top of the chimney was still securely fastened. No manager fancied climbing up the chimney to see how the job could be done better, so they were stuck. Then someone asked why the cowling was necessary. Lots of answers were offered, but none were convincing. So they looked up the history of the chimney and discovered that the cowling had been put in place in 1940 as part of wartime blackout regulations: it was to stop enemy bombers seeing the furnaces at the bottom of the chimney as they navigated their way to London. For 50 years, they had been sending a steeplejack to check that an unnecessary cowling was unnecessarily kept in place. The steeplejack returned one more time to remove the cowling, and then 100 per cent of the costs were removed.

- *Find the resources.* When you are told that someone does not have the time available to meet you, you know they are lying: they have the time, but you are not a priority. If they were offered $1 million and a hot date with their favourite sports or movie star, their very busy diary would suddenly become free. The same is true when you are told that no budget or staff are available for your agenda: you are being told a lie. There is always resource and budget if an idea is important and urgent enough. If your agenda is not urgent or important, find a different agenda to work on. If it is urgent and important, you can find the resource in one of two ways: you can ask for the resources (work the formal system) or you can engage your network of allies and supporters to help you (work the informal system).

> **There is always resource and budget if an idea is important and urgent enough**

Can you raise $2 billion a year?

STIR Education developed a powerful method for improving student performance by building the intrinsic motivation of teachers. It was a very low-cost intervention, costing just $3.30 per pupil per year. There was one small problem: the intervention was targeted at 600 million plus children which the

➤

UN had identified as being at school but not getting a proper education. That meant that the charity would have to raise $2 billion a year to address the scale of the problem. Becoming 5 per cent or 10 per cent or even 25 per cent more efficient would still leave an insurmountable fundraising gap for the charity. Charging for the intervention was not possible, because STIR works with some of the poorest countries which struggle to pay for textbooks and for teachers.

The solution has been to cut the cost by 90 per cent, with another 90 per cent cut to follow. Finding 90 per cent efficiency gains requires creative thinking. In this case, STIR realised that the programme will be even more effective if it is owned and delivered by each government. The programme has been redesigned to become part of how officials, teachers and training colleges work so that there is no extra cost to the government. With government taking delivery responsibility, 90 per cent of the costs disappear and quality goes up.

If you can work through people and partners you do not control, you work with all the resources you need. Work smarter, not harder.

5. I don't belong

Every firm is a tribe which is made up of many smaller tribes. The smaller tribes are defined by their function and their seniority. As with all tribes, they have their dress code, their rituals, their beliefs, their ways of talking and their ways of being. None of these tribal codes or beliefs are written down anywhere. You have to work them out for yourself. Try wearing a suit and tie in a tech start-up in Silicon Valley, and you will very quickly discover that you do not belong: casual dress is a rule just as much as formal dress is a rule elsewhere.

The positive reason these tribes exist is that it makes it easier to communicate: everyone understands the unwritten rules; they understand what is being said and what is not being said. The negative reason tribes exist is to exclude people who do not belong. But this is not a story about you: it is a story about them and their beliefs and rituals.

Tribal firms are a disaster for people who come from a different culture to the firm. If you come from a minority group, you will find it hard to decipher the code of the tribe, and even harder to adapt your behaviour to theirs. The reality is that you have to adapt to the firm, because the firm will not adapt to you. Firms preach diversity but practice conformity: you can be of any gender, ethnicity or religion as long as you sign up to the tribal way of thinking, acting and behaving.

> **Firms preach diversity but practice conformity**

Find the tribe where you want to belong and you will thrive.

6. I am not good enough

This is a crippling story to tell yourself, because it ensures that you never achieve your potential. If you believe you are not good enough, you will not seek the promotion, or chase that brilliant idea you had because you doubt yourself.

The reality is no one is ever good enough. No leader gets ticks in all the boxes. You don't need ticks in all the boxes either, because leadership is a team sport. You do not need to be great at everything. You need to build a team which will be great for you.

> **Leadership is a team sport**

'I am not good enough' is deficit thinking: if you look for weaknesses, you will always find them. Instead of looking for your weaknesses, look for your strengths. Your signature strengths are your key to success: find the context where your strengths will make the most difference.

> **Focus on your strengths, not your weaknesses**

Focus on your strengths, not your weaknesses.

Promoting inequality

We started Future Leaders to fast-track promising teachers into headship roles in disadvantaged areas, where they could make the most difference. It worked, sort of. We were able to identify, train and develop cohorts of teachers who became great head teachers. But there was a problem. After five years, we realised that over 80 per cent of the teachers who became heads were male, whereas we recruited gender-balanced cohorts which reflected the gender balance of the profession. We needed to find out what was going wrong.

Inevitably, we uncovered both overt and covert sexism in some of the school selection panels. But that was a relatively minor problem which affected a few schools. The bigger problem was the behaviour of our cohorts.

Usually, the males would start applying for headships when we knew that they were perhaps only 50–60 per cent ready. They believed that they would learn on the job successfully. If they were rejected, they would assume that the selection panel was made up of fools who made a mistake. Like a door-to-door salesman, they would keep knocking on school doors until they got accepted.

The females liked to wait until they were at least 90 per cent ready for headship. If they got rejected, they would take the feedback from the selection panel seriously. They would work on whatever weakness the panel had made up as a story to justify the rejection. When presented with these findings, the females first got angry and then got even: they started applying more often and earlier and they succeeded.

Believing you are not good enough is a great way to hobble your own career.

7. I must not fail

Once again, school teaches us the wrong lessons. We are taught that we must not fail. This is then translated into the business world as the search for excellence. We are expected to excel and never fail. That makes excellence the enemy of learning.

If we never fail, we never take risks. But that means we never learn and grow, and the firm never develops. If you are content to survive, you can avoid taking risks: you will not go anywhere, but you will be relatively safe until the next round of restructuring comes around. If you are to succeed, not just survive, you need to take risks: come up with ideas, create a new agenda, start a new initiative, step up in the crisis. Taking risk requires a different mindset:

- *Abundance versus poverty mindset*: The very poor cannot afford to take risks, because failure can be catastrophic. If you have abundance, you can afford occasional setbacks. At work, the abundance mindset is about recognising that there are endless opportunities to shine, especially if you create those opportunities. The poverty mindset believes that there are limited opportunities: if you win, I lose. The abundance mindset is collaborative and risk taking; the poverty mindset is competitive and risk averse. You choose.

- *Growth mindset*: Every setback is an opportunity to learn. The more you learn, the better you become. Successful entrepreneurs often have a string of failures to their name: each failure has helped them learn how to do better until they eventually succeed. You never fail, you just learn a little faster than you expected.

- *Success mindset*: A door-to-door salesperson knocked on my door and asked if I wanted to buy some overpriced kitchen goods. Before closing the door on them, I asked how he managed to keep going when so many doors get shut in his face. With a smile he replied, 'I reckon to sell to one or two doors in every one hundred. So I know that when you shut the door on me, I will be one door nearer to success. . . .' Successful managers can be like the door-to-door salesperson: they reframe failure. They tell themselves a story where they never fail. After yet another setback, one manager turned to me and said, 'It's OK, we haven't succeeded. . . yet'. Failure is not absolute, it is about timing: we have not succeeded, yet, and we may have to take a slight deviation on our way to success. Failure is just a stepping stone to success.

> **Failure is just a stepping stone to success**

8. Politics is a dirty business and not for me

All management involves the acquisition and use of power. In the past, power was mainly the formal power that came from your position: bigger budget, bigger teams and more decision-making rights. The message of *Impact* is that formal power helps, but is not enough. You have to amplify

> **Management involves the acquisition and use of power**

your formal power with informal power to make things happen through people you do not control. This puts politics at the heart of the management challenge. You have to make the organisation you work for, work for you.

Politics is like the Force in *Star Wars*: it can be used for good or for ill. If you believe that politics is all about back stabbing and sharp elbows then you are right to avoid it. That sort of politics will ensure you lose influence and allies. The positive form of politics is about creating the right networks of trust and influence to make great things happen. Understanding power and politics liberates you from the constraints of the traditional hierarchy. It allows you to achieve far more, regardless of what your formal job title may be. It is a force which is good for you and great for your firm.

Politics and PQ (political quotient) is the skill which managers need to thrive in the 21st century. It sits alongside the two traditional skill sets of IQ (19th century) and EQ (20th century). These three skill sets, combined with the mindset of success, are the keys to making impact and achieving more with less.

Building these skill sets and mind-sets makes management more challenging, and more rewarding, than ever. This is a world where you can shape your journey and control your

Whatever your journey may be, enjoy it

destiny. *Impact* is your guide not only to achieving more, but to finding more purpose and fulfilment on your journey through work and life. Whatever your journey may be, enjoy it.

Acknowledgements

One of the big lessons from *Impact* is that givers, not takers, are most likely to succeed. Only givers build the networks of trust and support you need to make things happen: takers can win battles by being selfish, but they lose the war by losing allies, influence and support. I have been immensely lucky to have encountered many givers who have given me their time, experience and support.

I want to thank all the generous executives who agreed to share their stories in this book including: Kate Adams, Tarek Alami, Børge Andreassen, Ed Beckingham, Paul Bennett, Alan Casey, Steve Cutts, Fiona Dawson, Mike Elliott, Walter Emberger, Mark Evans, Richard Grabinger, Noemi Hernandez Guerrero, Alastair Higginbottom, Russell Hobby, Steve Isherwood, Sharath Jeevan, Giouliana Kadra, Janthana Kaenprakhamroy, Fatima Koumbarji, Mehnaz Khan, Tia Lendo, Marco Maccari, Sally Maier-Yip, Lou McCrimlisk, Sri Chandana Nagoji, Kat Narayanan, Kenji Ota, Natasha Porter, Niven Postma, Vikas Pota, Tom Ravenscroft, Nicola Reindorp, John Rendel, Rebecca Robins, Adam Smith, David Stephen, Maddy Storr, Doug Strycharczyk, Cade Tan, Amanda Timberg, Nancy De Vore, William Wan, Jo Youle and Asrif Yusoff.

Where I refer to their job titles, I use the titles they had at the time of the interview: over time they will all move on to even greater things and their titles will change.

This book would simply not have been possible without the immense support of Pearson, who have been publishing my work for more than 20 years. In particular, I am grateful to my long-term editor Eloise Cook who saw the potential in this new topic, and to Amer Parikh who works wonders in bringing the book to market.

Finally, I am forever indebted to Hiromi who once again became a temporary book widow while I disappeared into a writing shell for some months.

As ever, if there are any mistakes in this book they are all mine.

Index